Endorsements

Mary Dyer, an ordained minister, connects her unique experience in two invisible communities—(a) as a near-deaf hearing advocate and (b) a lesbian—to the history and life experience of deaf and LGBT people. With her creative blend of memoir, informative narrative, and religious insight, Dyer sheds light on both worlds.

David G. Myers, Hope College,
author of *A Quiet World: Living with Hearing Loss* and
What God Has Joined Together: The Christian Case for Gay Marriage

---

Mary's book *Walls or Windows: Are the Deaf and LGBT Communities "Wholly Other" or "Holy Other"?* uniquely describes the intersection of her own life as a deaf person who also identifies as LGBT. Her personal background brings authenticity to her arguments and the primary—and optimistic—thesis of the book. Moreover, her seamless comingling of these seemingly disparate groups provides readers with notions likely to challenge long-held views among many. Her well-researched overview of the political, legal, and sociological struggles and triumphs relative to both groups over time is informative and compelling. The many profiles of theologians, historians, activists, poets, and writers will provide readers with additional perspectives.

Carol S. Lomicky, Professor Emerita of Journalism,
University of Nebraska at Kearney

I am pleased to see how the work of Emmanuel Levinas and my class, "The Allergy to the Other," have significantly inspired Mary Dyer's writing so many years after we worked together. This is what I always hope to do as an educator: generate interests that will inspire students and support them in their future professional and personal lives. Mary integrates autobiographical storytelling, history, theologies, justice work, and the arts as they relate to the themes of otherness and othering in relation to the LGBTQ and deaf communities. She invites readers to take a deep journey with her, leading them with grace through well-researched and thoughtful chapters that contribute to form a vibrant tapestry of learning.

Rev. Dr. Gabriella Lettini, former dean of the
Star King School for the Ministry in Berkeley, California

Reminding me of the duality of Amphisbaena, the two-headed serpent in ancient Greek and Roman legend, Mary Dyer's *Walls or Windows* examines two different challenges she has faced in her life—hearing loss and a gay orientation. Exacerbated by sudden loss of her hearing rather than the typical gradual decline in hearing acuity, her midlife awareness and acceptance of her gay orientation makes her experience somewhat unique. Mary explores many aspects of the gay experience, covering a wide range of topics including historical events, cultural shifts, personal narratives, and the evolution of LGBTQ+ rights and representation. Interwoven with that discussion is a presentation of the experiences and thoughts of a person with severe hearing loss. Learning about the diverse experiences faced by people with either or both of these challenges will foster greater understanding and create a sense of empathy and connection within readers.

Stephen Frazier, freelance writer and Head of Loop New Mexico

"Intersectionality" is a term used in the social sciences to describe overlapping social, cultural, and political identities. We all, to some extent, manage multiple different identities, but few of us have to navigate more than one social identity that is the target of extreme—and extremely ignorant—hateful stigma. In a matter-of-fact voice that belies her exemplary bravery, Mary Dyer describes her personal journey in *Walls or Windows*, an extended meditation on the Deaf and LGBT communities and their impact on her own identity. Combining autobiography, poetry, the history of deafness, gay pride, Christian theology, and philosophical exegesis that concludes with an Epistemology of Hope, Dyer's book is a moving deep-dive into how her passionately lived identities are constructed, how they have been portrayed, and how those portrayals have shaped her life.

Richard Einhorn, composer and hearing loss advocate

WALLS or WINDOWS

Are the Deaf and LGBT Communities "Wholly Other" or "Holy Other"?

Mary Heron Dyer

© 2025
Published in the United States by Nurturing Faith, Macon, GA.
Nurturing Faith is a book imprint of Good Faith Media (goodfaithmedia.org).
Library of Congress Cataloging-in-Publication Data is available.

ISBN: 978-1-63528-258-0

All rights reserved. Printed in the United States of America.

Scripture quotations marked (KJV) are taken from the King James Version, 1611, public domain.

Scripture quotations marked (NIV) are taken from the Holy Bible, New International Version®, NIV® Copyright ©1973, 1978, 1984, 2011 by Biblica, Inc.® Used by permission. All rights reserved worldwide.

Scripture quotations marked (NRSV) are taken from the New Revised Standard Version, Updated Edition. Copyright © 2021 National Council of Churches of Christ in the United States of America. Used by permission. All rights reserved worldwide.

Contents

Foreword 1

Introduction 3

Chapter 1: Overlapping Issues of the Deaf and LGBT Communities 4

Chapter 2: The Framework: Levinas and Thurman 6

Chapter 3: An Overview of Parallels Between the Deaf and LGBT
    Communities 12

Chapter 4: Membership 15

Chapter 5: Popular Media Portrayals of the Deaf 19

Chapter 6: Popular Portrayals of Gays in the Media 25

Chapter 7: A Brief History of the Deaf Community in the US before
    "The Revolution" 40

Chapter 8: LGBT History in the United States before Stonewall
    in 1969 48

Chapter 9: Psychological and Medical Treatments before the
    Revolutions 65

Chapter 10: Horizontal Oppression and "Passing" 77

Chapter 11: Stonewall and After: The Match that Ignited a Revolution,
    June 27, 1969 81

Chapter 12: The Deaf Revolution: Gallaudet and "Deaf President Now!"
    March 6, 1988 86

Chapter 13: Current Educational, Medical, and Legal Issues:
    Who Decides for the Deaf? 90

Chapter 14: Current Educational, Medical, and Legal Issues:
    Who Decides for LGBT? 101

Chapter 15: Some Major "Queer" Theological Ideas and Theologians 117

Chapter 16: Theologies of Disability 129

Chapter 17: Beginning Considerations in Theologies of the Deaf 133

Chapter 18: A Theology of The Deaf—
    The Work of Wayne Morris and Hannah Lewis 139

Conclusion: An Epistemology of Hope 159

Bibliography 162

Foreword

I realize that the title I chose for this book is mysterious. Read the lyrics of the song "Walls and Windows" by Judy Small, a popular Australian songwriter and singer, and you will understand a bit better.

> Walls and Windows (Performed by Judy Small in 1985)
> Did you sing your children lullabies to calm their fears at night?
> Did you hold them gently till they went to sleep?
> Did you plant in them the seeds of hope for new and better lives?
> Did you make them promises you couldn't keep?
> Do you think of me as enemy and could you call me friend?
> Or will we let our differences destroy us in the end
> The wall that stands between us could be a window too
> When I look into the mirror I see you
> And do you have sons who fight for peace the way I'm told mine do?
> Do they send you photographs from foreign lands?
> Do you chill to see the missiles, and do they haunt your dreams?
> Do you wonder whose the power, whose the hands?
> Do you think of me as enemy and could you call me friend?
> Or will we let our differences destroy us in the end
> The wall that stands between us could be a window too
> When I look into the mirror I see you
> Oh may we live to see the day when walls of words and fear
> No longer stand between the truth and dreams
> When walls of windows rise into the darkness and we dare
> To look into the mirror and see peace
> Do you think of me as enemy and could you call me friend?
> Or will we let our differences destroy us in the end
> The wall that stands between us could be a window too
> When I look into the mirror I see you
> When I look into the mirror I see you[1]

Judy Small presents the invitation of this book. When we encounter people who are different from us, do we build windows to be able to see through to each other, to allow ourselves to be changed by our interaction, or do we build walls to shut off anything and anyone that does not "fit in"—to our culture, religious views, politics, skin color, ableism, or sexual identity? The cover photo is meant to be ambiguous. Is the wall slowly being broken down, or just in need, yet again, of repair?

In the United States of the early 2000s, we favor walls so much that one administration even tried to build an "unbreachable" wall to separate the United States from Mexico. Many people still believe this crumbling and unfinished wall can keep out the "others" whom they find intimidating: Mexicans, anyone with brown skin color, the poor, those who do not speak English, and the exclusionary list goes on. Judy's song challenges all of us to dream a different dream.

This song holds the key to the challenge, the invitation, of this book. It is a natural human response to react in fear when we encounter something we have not experienced before, including people who seem different. We are born into a tribe, a family, and a culture that shelters us and indoctrinates us until we are bodily and emotionally ready to build our own unique lives, keeping what is worthy and discarding what no longer serves us.

It takes a lot of courage to expand our boundaries, question our beliefs, and step away from the small cocoon that initially kept us safe but now holds us a bit too tightly and binds our budding wings.

It is my hope and intent that this book will invite you, challenge you, and even offend you in places. May it help you take a new look at what you have welcomed and what you have shut out. Part of this process involves undermining the usually benevolent looking but ultimately poisonous colonialism that sees "success" only when it erases the differences of the "other" until we can safely accept them as looking, speaking, and believing enough like us to welcome them into our tribe.

Note

[1] Judy Small, "Walls and Windows," *One Voice in the Crowd*, ©1984 Crafty Maid Music/Pat Humphries. Words used by permission.

Introduction

It has been intriguing to juxtapose these two minority communities—the LGBT (lesbian, gay, bisexual, transgender) and the Deaf—something I would never have conceived of if they had not intersected in my own life. I came out as a lesbian at the age of forty, which necessitated my leaving a twenty-year marriage and thus having to co-parent three children (ages seven, fourteen, and sixteen) from separate residences.

For years, this coming out process dominated my existence, thrust me from gainful employment in the Catholic church, sent me into a spiritual wilderness, and gradually led me back to the center—perhaps not the "center" of a society based on prejudice and discrimination against various groups perceived outside the pale but to my own center. During those years, I integrated my sexuality with my other life experiences and values, and, while I never completely abandoned the continuing quest for inclusion, it became only one of many traits that describe me.

Then, without warning, I became deaf overnight following routine surgery in May 2008. This led me to another unanticipated journey on my life path. Having studied about and lived daily the life of a "sexual minority" for more than two decades, I had a framework in which to explore and understand some interrelated issues between the Deaf community and the LGBT experience. When I speak of the Deaf experience in this book, I am not referring to hard-of-hearing or even late-deafened, which is how I identify myself, but to those born deaf and those who consider themselves "culturally deaf." This means that they belong to the Deaf community and use American Sign Language as their single mode of communication. Although some of them can talk, most of them do not seem to want to. I learned this firsthand when I served on the Iowa Board for the Deaf. At meetings, I would use my cochlear implant and read the captioning as needed, but all of the deaf board members would sign so that the signer would speak what they were signing to the rest of us.

Chapter 1
Overlapping Issues of the Deaf and LGBT Communities

It is a strange juxtaposition to put LGBT people and deaf people together, sort of like putting an elephant's nose on a giraffe. It took me a long time to see how well these two communities intersect, despite what a casual glance might reveal. I "came out" in 1986, but losing my hearing in May 2008 after elective knee replacement rocked my world, changing how I felt about myself and raising the question of how and if I could or would want to survive if my hearing did not come back. I even wondered if this might be some cruel cosmic joke.

Immediately I sank into deep depression as the sounds around me were tantalizingly out of reach, feeling like the original Tantalus, an Olympian god who had offended the higher-ups. His punishment was to be forever up to his neck in a lake, and whenever he tried to bend his head to drink, the water would recede. (He might have deserved this since he murdered his own son and tried to trick the other gods into eating him.) I wondered how I could live as a spectator to my own life, trying to figure out even the simplest conversations, tantalizingly within my sight but not entering my "dead" ears. Every day in my hospital bed, I wrote in my journal and turned to poetry to ponder the purpose of life itself.

My moods swung wildly between each rising and setting of the sun, and poems flowed into me. My bed was on the seventh floor, with the inaccessible, reinforced window looking out over San Francisco Bay. It seemed that the birds were singing to me, but I could not hear them. One day I hoped to once again sit on my front porch and listen to the birds sing. But it was not to be that day.

The Birds Are Singing...Somewhere
Mary Heron Dyer
May 28, 2008, early morning...a new poem

Each morning I awake
I lie expectant in the darkness
Hoping against hope
the birds whose cheerful trills rise
up on the bright crisp morning air
to greet the dawn outside my window
are real—
and not just a sad mixture of memory and hope,
served up to me, before breakfast,

a dreary daily dose of spiritual discipline,
bran flakes for the soul.
And yet if this is yet to be
just another day—imposed or given—
in silence
can I lift it with the song of my heart?

For decades, the Deaf and LGBT communities were invisible. The deaf were sent to Deaf schools, separated from their families, forbidden to use sign, and taught how to speak and read lips to at least try to fit into the hearing world. By and large, however, they were consigned to workshops like shoe factories and newspaper print shops, where they had no connection to the hearing community and thus became protective of one another in their other-imposed isolation. The gay community (we gained the other cognomens—lesbian, bisexual, transgender, queer—at later dates) survived by staying hidden and discreet. Otherwise, we could be imprisoned, lose our jobs, or even be sent to psychiatric facilities for horrific "treatments" intended to change our sexual identity.

Dozens of issues, all tangled up together, relate to both the Deaf and LGBT communities. This book is an overview of these similar issues. In addition, it invites the reader to consider a new framework in which to view the "other." Are they the "Wholly Other," where the dominant paradigm is either to annihilate or assimilate into certain standards and beliefs? Or might they provide, as Emmanuel Levinas and Howard Thurman both suggest,[1] a way to encounter the "Holy Other"—to stand face to face on holy ground, not consumed by the other but enriched by the passion of Love that reveals our connection through embracing our differences?

It was tempting to title this book *Maybe Dick: In Search of the Great White Male*. Obviously, this is a nod to Herman Melville's great nineteenth-century American classic, *Moby Dick*, which portrays Captain Ahab's relentless hunt for this great white whale. In the book, Ahab, the captain of a whaler, is obsessed with hunting down the almost mythical and certainly mystical white whale who took away his leg in their previous fateful encounter. Melville wrote of Ahab, "His hair is disheveled, his face is furrowed, and there is a fever in his blood that only the conquest of the white whale can cure. In effect, he says to the lightning, 'You may destroy this vessel, you may dry up the bowels of the sea, you may consume me; but I can still be ashes.'"[2] The "other," in this case represented by the great white whale, is perceived as so threatening to Ahab that the captain is consumed by it to the point of fatalistically being compelled to bring about his own destruction in its attainment.

The United States of America is often referred to as "the melting pot," with the concomitant although not totally conscious belief that, once someone travels to these shores, the task of assimilation immediately begins. Chopp and Taylor summarize it succinctly:

> One of the dominant metaphors for the United States has been that of the society as a melting pot. In the myth of the melting pot, Americans supposedly shed their cultural particularities, their ethnic differences, their special languages and customs. The melting pot myth promised that if people left all such particularities behind, they could succeed, that is, they could become ideal Americans. This ideal American was imaged as a white Anglo-Saxon Protestant male who had a domestic wife and several children, who spoke without an accent, and who worked hard and was handsomely rewarded.[3]

Defined that way, "assimilation" routinely becomes—sometimes only subconsciously—a process chillingly like annihilation, whereby anything a little too "different" or "foreign" needs to be erased, if not simply by the process of assimilation itself then perhaps, as a last recourse, by laws of exclusion. One need only scan newspapers and recent court cases to see the desire of the "many" to legally erase the right of "minorities" to access information in their own native tongues. This right was not established by the Supreme Court until 1974, as a natural outgrowth of the Civil Rights Act the same year. The ruling, in a unanimous decision, landed in favor of bilingual instruction to help non-native English-speaking students improve their English language competency.

If current immigration and birthrate trends continue their current course and if a linguistic "minority" becomes a "majority" of the population, one might well wonder could "they" not then enact laws making it illegal to use English in "our" workplace? It's an interesting idea. Then one group could just trade places with the other group, and the deadly assimilation/annihilation dance could go on ad infinitum…or perhaps, more fittingly, ad nauseam. What would the world look like, however, if the "other" were invited in as an honored guest, an equal partner, with their own gifts to bring to the banquet of life, rather than feared and hated?

Notes

[1] Howard Thurman, *Jesus and the Disinherited* (Boston: Beacon Press, 1996), 80.
[2] Herman Melville, *Moby Dick* (Harper and Brothers, 1851), 1.
[3] Rebecca Chopp and Mark Lewis Taylor, eds., *Reconstructing Christian Theology* (Minneapolis: Fortress Press, 1997), 3.

Chapter 2
The Framework: Levinas and Thurman

The main thesis of philosophers Emmanuel Levinas and Howard Thurman is that whenever one group was introduced to another group, their first reaction was usually distrust and a sense of being threatened, not interest in what the new group might bring to benefit all. I had my own experience of the process of dismantling the "Othering" of gay people in June 1992. At the time, I lived in Oregon and had just finished my master's in counseling at Oregon State University in Corvallis.

Homophobia was at its height then, and my five classmates, who would return to their public classrooms upon completing their degrees, had to hide their sexuality to preserve their employment status. I planned to go into agency counseling, where I would be able to live out the wholeness of who I was.

Two resolutions were coming up for a statewide vote in the next election, and I felt the need to address them. I had to do something. The most offensive and egregious one linked bestiality with homosexuality. The other one outlawed necrophilia. They were both aimed at the gay community.[1] The protest that most appealed to me was called "The Walk Against Hate: The Walk for Love and Justice." The two-week walk was planned to go from Eugene to Portland, where we would arrive in time to lead the "Gay Pride" parade in June, right behind the Dykes on Bikes. It was around 150 miles, and we would stay at various host sites each night. We packed as little as we needed, with our backpacks carried by the lead car (the one with a portable toilet in the back, which I occasionally had to use!). It was right behind the driver, a male Metropolitan Community Church pastor. We stayed at churches, private homes, a senior center, a county fairground, a United Farm Worker Hall, and a university. A variety of allies delivered lunches at our rest stops, including a spontaneous visit by a follower of our radio updates who drove up with a cooler full of ice cream! Measure 9, included below, was the focus of our protest during this walk.[2]

Oregon Ballot Measure 9

Be it Enacted by the People by the State of Oregon:

Paragraph 1. The Constitution of the State of Oregon is amended by creating a new section to be added to and made a part of Article I and to read:

Section

1. This state shall not recognize any categorical provision such as "sexual orientation," "sexual preference," and similar phrases that include homosexuality, pedophilia, sadism or masochism. Quotas, minority status,

affirmative action, or any similar concepts, shall not apply to these forms of conduct, nor shall government promote these behaviors.

2. State, regional and local governments and their properties and monies shall not be used to promote, encourage, or facilitate homosexuality, pedophilia, sadism or masochism.

3. State, regional and local governments and their departments, agencies and other entities, including specifically the State Department of Higher Education and the public schools, shall assist in setting a standard for Oregon's youth that recognizes homosexuality, pedophilia, sadism and masochism as abnormal, wrong, unnatural, and perverse and that these behaviors are to be discouraged and avoided.

4. It shall be considered that it is the intent of the people enacting this section that if any part thereof is held unconstitutional, the remaining parts shall be held in force.

To become marchers, we had to take nonviolent training and agree to its principles. The walk was open to anyone with good will, but the core group was lesbians. Those of us who identified as homosexual had fought hard for our rights, for our jobs, in our families, and in our churches—if we still had one. Most of us, like me, had left church as we were viewed as "sinners" to be somehow converted to heterosexuality. Thus, we were at first protective and defensive. Our worldview at the beginning of the march was that our experience as the "Other" was hurtful, harmful, hateful, and hostile.

For the long walk about to begin, I had my grandmother's Bible in my backpack and a small American flag tucked into my belt. I had been forced out of both my religion and my country and church, and I chose to reclaim my rightful membership during this march. Like my fellow marchers, I expected resistance and rebuke. What we discovered, however, was a whole host of allies giving their time, their love, their shelter, and their stories, all of them eager to hear our stories and become even stronger allies. The walls came tumbling down, a brick at a time, until there was no "Other" at all but a deep mutual respect and growing love.

Perhaps the most powerful night was when we slept on the floor at the United Farm Workers Hall in Woodburn. At the evening program, our side was all white and mostly lesbian and gay, and the other side was male farm workers from Guatemala and Mexico. So there we were—white and brown, male and female, Hispanic and Anglo, us mostly middle class and the others poor, both English speaking and Spanish speaking. Through the interpreter and through sharing our personal stories of tragedy and triumph, we "listened" one another into life.[3] By the end of our time there, we had committed to continue our connection with these men. The "Wholly Other" had become the "Holy Other."

Ballot measure 9 was ultimately defeated. There were 638,527 votes yes and 828,290 votes no—43.52% yes, 56.47% no. I believe our walk and other peaceful resistance and protests won the day, but as I write in 2025, we have still not won the battle.

On a personal note, I missed the last day of walking the Burnside Bridge across the Willamette River into downtown Portland. I had contracted "walking pneumonia" the day before and had to go to the ER for treatment. My partner drove me across the bridge the next day so I could take my place against the other marchers, right behind the Dykes on Bikes!

Anyone over a certain age would be able to identify this line, "Just the facts, ma'am," first from the radio and then the later TV show *Dragnet* with Jack Webb as its producer and star. Yet "facts" take on a life of their own, especially when they cover emotionally charged issues. The place and role of the outsider—whatever group is being targeted—evokes strong feelings that make "facts" virtually vanish in a puff of smoke or get covered with a smokescreen by one side or the other in their often-acrimonious debates. While this certainly applies to both groups I address in this book, the Deaf community and the LGBT community, it is essentially true of all minority groups in their discourse with the majority. Thus it is imperative to look behind the "facts," to be transparent and consistent in delineating how one is to hold the "facts."

The ideas of two theologians form the framework of my approach, offering us a view of the other as "Holy Other" rather than "Wholly Other." The first is Emmanuel Levinas (1906–1995), a Lithuanian philosopher and Talmudic scholar. The second is Howard Thurman (1899–1981), an African American theologian, prophet, and mystic whose witness and writings strongly impacted Martin Luther King Jr. as King lit a fire under the Civil Rights Movement of the 1960s. Each of them provides a refreshingly different and complementary framework with which to view "otherness."

Emmanuel Levinas was a both a philosopher and Talmudic commentator. Becoming a French citizen in 1930, he was conscripted in World War II, captured, and spent most of the war in a German prisoner of war camp. While Levinas's wife and daughter were hidden in a monastery during the war, other members of his extended family were slaughtered by the Nazi war machine, so he brings a truly personal, indeed visceral, experience to his reflections on the "Other." In a nutshell, Levinas turned traditional philosophies on their heads by claiming that personal ethical responsibility to others must be both the starting point and the primary focus for philosophy. Ethics thus preempted ontology (the fixed, unchangeable nature of being). This line of thought resembles Martin Buber's idea of "I and Thou" but with more emphasis on a relationship of respect and responsibility for the other person rather than a relationship of mutuality and dialogue.

In *Totality and Infinity: An Essay on Exteriority*, Levinas claims "infinity is produced in the relationship of the same with the other." Even more important is that this relationship to the other needs to be "…welcoming the Other as hospitality," and in this "…the idea of infinity is consummated." Then Levinas outlines two basic approaches to the "Other": the first is one of absorption, and, in contrast, the second is not annihilation but radical hospitality that is open to the possibility of a face-to-face encounter, which changes both parties. In absorption, he states that "I can 'feed' on these realities [of the Other] and to a very great extent satisfy myself, as though I had simply been lacking them. Their *alterity* is thereby reabsorbed into my own identity as a thinker or a possessor."[4]

Anyone familiar with American colonial history can understand this first approach, with our treatment both of Indigenous peoples, whose land was systematically and brutally stolen, and of African slaves, brought in to clear the forests, till the fields, and provide white masters with personal service, including total control over both their kinship groups and even their own bodies. Yet Levinas holds out a higher, second vision, one that is perhaps not so much about the "Other" but about ourselves if we can open up to the possibility of encountering the "Other" on holy ground:

> The metaphysical desire tends toward *something else entirely*, toward the *absolutely other*…. The metaphysical desire does not long to return, for it is desire for a land not of our birth, for a land foreign to every nature, which has not been our fatherland and to which we shall never betake ourselves. The metaphysical desire does not rest upon any prior kinship. It is a desire that cannot be satisfied.

Levinas further claims that there is another intention of metaphysical desire—the Desired does not fulfill it but deepens it. If we pursue this second dialogue, there is a conundrum he presents, asking how can the same, wrapped in egoism, enter into a relationship with the other that does not take away the other's alterity. If it does, he asks what the nature of the new relationship is. His conclusion is at once a bit frightening, as we step away from our egoism and superiority that is mostly enforced by various forms of violence, and at the same time exciting and transforming, as we enter the sacred space of honoring the new knowledge that we are not both the same and the other.

In a later book, *Ethics and Infinity*, Levinas develops this theme by stating unequivocally that the "true union or true togetherness is not a togetherness of synthesis, but a togetherness of *face to face*."[5] For him the crucial consideration is "to know if society in the current sense of the term is the result of a limitation of the principle that men are predators of one another, or if to the contrary it results from the limitation of the principle that men are *for* one another."

Preacher, prophet, and mystic Howard Thurman also had a personal investment in his own theological work. Born in 1899 in a legally segregated America, he was raised by a grandmother who had been a slave. In his first major work, *Jesus and the Disinherited*, first published in 1949, Thurman uses Jesus as a model of how the oppressed (with Jesus it was the Jews living under Roman occupation, and with Thurman it was African Americans living under Jim Crow laws) need to face not only their oppression but also their oppressors.[6] He claims that to love the enemy must mean that a fundamental attack must first be made on status, that each person, oppressor and oppressed, must break out of those limiting roles to emerge as people.

His co-founding of the Church for the Fellowship of All Peoples in San Francisco in 1944, in the wake of the forced interning of Japanese and Japanese Americans during World War II, was his concrete answer to the threatening "Otherness" of those groups that were disenfranchised at the time. The church itself, three-quarters of a century later, is still practicing the principles that Thurman and Dr. Fisk, the white co-pastor, put in place so many years ago in the midst of a world war.

For now, I will put aside the foundational work of these two men, returning to them to draw on their and others' insights at the conclusion. Let us focus on the two objects of this paper, the Deaf and LGBT communities, to see some of their commonalties.

Notes

[1] It was years later that that the gay community was expanded first to include lesbians, then bisexuals, transsexuals, and queer, with others still emerging.

[2] "1992 Oregon Ballot Measure 9," *Wikipedia*, https://en.wikipedia.org/wiki/1992_Oregon_Ballot_Measure_9; "Measure 9 (1992)," *Oregon State University*, https://guides.library.oregonstate.edu/politicsandpolicies/Measure9.

[3] I learned this concept by reading *The Journey Is Home* by Nelle Morton (Beacon Press, 1985). It has become the center of my own spiritual practice when listening to others.

[4] Emmanuel Levinas, *Totality and Infinity: An Essay on Exteriority* (Pittsburgh, PA: Duquesne University Press, 1969). Until noted otherwise, all quotes from Levinas below are from this source.

[5] Emmanuel Levinas, *Ethics and Infinity: Conversations with Philippe Nemo*, trans. Richard A. Cohen (Pittsburgh: Duquesne University Press, 1995).

[6] Howard Thurman, *Jesus and the Disinherited* (Boston: Beacon Press, 1996), 80.

Chapter 3
An Overview of Parallels Between the Deaf and LGBT Communities

Soon after I was discharged by the hospital after my rather eventful knee surgery in May 2008, I was not yet physically able to stay by myself in the apartment we had at the seminary, along with our four dogs and one cat who needed care. Sheryl, my spouse, who was working on her MDiv at Pacific School of Religion in Berkeley, California, on her way to ordination as a Disciple of Christ, had an opportunity to go to a Native American reservation in eastern Washington state to do some research on their history, so I got to tag along.

We were the only ones in the bunk-bed room on the second floor, but she was busy all day with her research, and we also had no internet service. Unfortunately, the bathroom was downstairs and across from the large dining room. Several times a day I had to hang on to the railing as I cautiously descended the stairs and then used a cane to cross the floor to the facilities. One day Sheryl was down there talking with an intern, but I could neither hear anything nor get even a wave as a greeting. I was virtually invisible. Thus, this poem was born.

Shelf Life
Mary Heron Dyer

Shelf life is great, if you're a can of corn
tucked away in a closet.
The longer stored, the better,
insurance against floods and famines.

But what if you're someone just
sidelined by sudden hearing loss?
Tucked away among the beans and spinach?

Silent, silenced,
I look out on human contact,
So near but far away, now for me a one-sided
and decidedly unequal
game of charades,

Earless, I try to piece together
fragments of conversation,
captured from moving lips…

Decipher body language,
random hand gestures.

Spirits sagging,
tired from the strain,
defeated by the hearing world,
I shut my eyes. Holding back unshed tears.
On the whole, I'd rather be a can of corn.

I wrote this of course, during the early days of my deafness. While I was trying to learn sign language, I still did not know if my hearing would return naturally or if I might be eligible for a cochlear implant. Ultimately, I did get one, and it is obviously precious to me, but it still does not replace "natural" hearing. So yes, I am deaf, but I do not belong to the Deaf community. And yes, I can hear with my cochlear implant but must struggle every day both with difficult hearing situations and with a hearing community that neither recognizes my hearing loss nor has any impulse, for the most part, to make those of us with hearing loss welcome, even though we are around 20 percent of the population. It is especially galling for me, as I have found my way back into the Christian community and become an ordained member of the Christian Church (Disciples of Christ), that so many churches proudly proclaim on their outside signs, "All are Welcome!" Most of them, if they are honest, need to put an asterisk after the "welcome" to say "but not those with hearing loss."

First, I would like to provide some definitions and limitations. This book is only a "sampler" of some of the main issues that I perceive linking the Deaf and LGBT communities. I am also dealing only with the United States as I address these issues. The "Deaf" to whom I refer are people culturally and/or born deaf, using American Sign Language as either their only or primary language. The LGBT community, which can justifiably now add "I" for "intersex" and "Q" for either "Queer" or "Questioning," is as complex as the constantly expanding acronym indicates. I will be writing only in generalities, which, by definition, cannot give the nuanced treatment this subject so richly deserves.

I believe several areas are crucial to understanding how these two seemingly disparate communities have similar issues, concerns, histories, triumphs, and ongoing challenges. The first is their *membership*. Unlike most other minority communities, which have cohesion based on birth and family status and connection, these two communities are largely formed by "accidents" of birth, both the born or early deafened children and LGBT children and adolescents who are probably being raised by those not like them. Most deaf children are born to hearing parents.

Most LGBT children are raised by heterosexual parents. This perhaps, more than any other, is a primary consideration to show their connectedness to each other.

Most deaf children not only belong to a different cultural group than their parents and must therefore be enculturated into this group through means other than their parents but also face the added barrier in that their primary language, ASL in this country, "differs not only in code structure but in channel structure from the majority language,"[1] effectively making language oppression doubly severe for deaf people. An added "twist" for those born deaf is that ASL is diglossic, meaning that there is signing deaf people use among themselves and another signing used when in communication with the hearing community, based mostly on those who see deafness as a medical pathology.

For the LGBT community, the path to authentic personhood is much more varied and takes a lot more time. The unfolding revelation of one's sexuality, of one's gender identity, sometimes takes many years, with the added or at least intensified onus of a different kind of "pathology," no longer medical perhaps, at least in the mainstream medical establishment, but with certain religious, cultural, and political groups. Membership is the first and probably most cogent factor linking the two communities, which leads us to a more detailed exposition in the following chapter.

Note

[1] James Woodward, *How You Gonna Get to Heaven If You Can't Talk with Jesus? On Depathologizing Deafness* (Silver Spring, MD: T. J. Publishers, Inc., 1982), 11.

Chapter 4
Membership

I am aware that I was lucky in the circumstances of my birth. I was the only child of white, middle-class parents. My father, after he got his textile engineering degree at Clemson College ("Go, Tigers!") for his service in World War II, went on to be part of the NASA team working on their first moon landing. In 1966, he helped find fabrics that would be used for the parachute on the landing module. My mother, decades after he died, got her BA in English literature on the GI bill too, as she had been a naval nurse in WWII.

I got to go to a private Catholic girls' high school, and it was assumed I would at least get my bachelor's degree. I admit I got carried away with education. I got my Master of Arts in English literature from UCSB in 1969, my MA in theology and scripture in 1979 from Mt. Angel Seminary in St. Benedict, Oregon (the first woman to graduate), and my Master of Science in counseling from Oregon State University in 1992. Then, in 2006 I finished a two-year graduate program at Unity School of Theology in Lee's Summit, Missouri, and got ordained a Unity minister. Finally, I received a graduate student "Certificate of Sexuality and Spirituality" at Pacific School of Religion in Berkeley, and the 146-page paper I wrote for that program has morphed into this book eighteen years later. I also have a two-year degree from a local community college in Horticulture. (I may not be finished yet.)

When my parents and I finally settled into our home in Palos Verdes Estates, California, in 1952, I had a secure life. I was a tomboy and enjoyed beating boys at arm wrestling. They would even knock on our door to ask me to come out and play touch football, where, by common consent, they would choose me as their quarterback because I had the strongest arm and most accurate spiral throw.

When I transferred to University of the Pacific in Stockton, California, in fall 1964, my mother insisted I go a week early for sorority rush. Faithfully I attended all their teas, dressed right—even wearing short white gloves—and behaved myself, making small talk about trivia, but it felt so artificial. Did my mother not yet realize that I would never fit the mold of a sorority girl? When I sat with the other candidates to open our envelopes, I was relieved that mine was empty. I could stop trying to pretend I was that kind of girl. I would get to be a sorority of one! My mother just needed to get over it, I thought. I had my own path.

I never fit the mold, even as an adult. The last time I wore a dress or used lipstick was at my daughter's wedding in 1998, only at her insistence. I even had to stop biting my nails months beforehand. I still like to challenge men to arm wrestling, and I usually win. This will go on until and if I get osteoarthritis. (I am still biting my nails, and I don't give a damn!)

As alluded to in chapter 3, membership in these two "select" groups, the Deaf community and the LGBT community, is by and large "happenstance." As I mulled over how to illustrate this, lyrics of a song from the Fantasticks, "Plant a Radish," by Will McMillan came to mind:

> While with progeny, it's hodge-podgeny, for as soon as
> You think you know what kind you've got, it's what they're not!"

The main point of the song is that when you plant a seed from a radish, it has to come up as a radish, but that is not the case with children. The writer is comparing the dependability of a seed growing into a particular kind of plant to the much chancier venture of "growing" children."

Even if potential parents understand this truth at an intellectual level, and perhaps even stretch their imaginations to encompass different shapes and sizes, personalities, and eye and hair color, most hearing parents who discover that their child is deaf or, usually later in the child's development, LGBT, have great difficulty understanding. Questions arise. Decisions must be made, and the most crucial one centers on that of belonging—or not.

Some studies have shown that at least 90 percent of deaf children are born to hearing parents. Others claim that it is even higher, that 96 percent of deaf children born in the United States are born to parents with normal hearing. While many, if not most, deaf parents not only welcome but actually hope for a deaf child, it is not so with hearing parents. The same holds true for the LGBT community, although the statistics are harder to verify and the coming out process is much lengthier. Many reputable studies claim that up to 10 percent of the population falls into the LGBT category. So the statistics are strikingly similar: 90 percent of deaf children being raised by hearing parents, 90 percent of LGBT children being raised by heterosexual parents.

This means these two communities—Deaf and LGBT—are outsiders in the larger community, sometimes even within their own families. Somehow some of them make it and are ultimately embraced by their loved ones, yet many are forced to find primary support communities outside of their birth families. Indeed, the metaphor for family, born or chosen, is fundamental and recurrent, but the salience of Deaf identity overshadows differences of age, class, sex, and ethnicity that would be of much more prominence in hearing society. *The Mask of Benevolence: Disabling the Deaf Community* elaborates on themes in much greater depth.[1]

It is a bit different in heterosexual families. The prejudice against gender-nonconforming children is delayed in most cases by two factors. The first is that it sometimes takes a few years for a child or young adult to understand that they have a gender identity different from the one with which they were raised.

The second is the many ways society has continued to have prejudice about and power over them. For instance, their rights to marry, to be employed, to buy a house, to get health care for their partner, to adopt…the list goes on and on. Unfortunately, the nation's new administration in 2025, as well as a growing number of states, are trying to enact or bring back laws that will drastically affect LGBT lives.

When interacting with these two communities, people must remember that they were formed in the fire of birth into deafness or, later, an exploration of their "minority" sexuality, hardened in the flames of family miscommunication and conflict, and refined by rubbing against one another to discover their brilliance. Continue to ponder the implications of those born deaf to hearing parents, a double oppression. They don't speak the same language or process information the same way. This is no minor distinction, but, while obvious to those born deaf, it is seemingly invisible to social scientists. Renowned social scientist Gordon Allport, for instance, said in 1954 that "There is one law—universal in all human societies…. In every society on earth the child is regarded as a member of his parents' groups. He belongs to the same race, stock, family tradition, religion, caste, and occupational status."[2] Douglas Baynton is charitable in evaluating Allport's unthinking stance:

> He was wrong, but it is hard to fault him. Deaf people occupy a unique position. They make up the only cultural group where cultural information and language has been predominantly passed down from child to child rather than from adult to child, and the only one in which the native language of the children is different from the language spoken by the parents. In schools for the deaf, children whose parents are deaf (about 10 percent of the total) teach the other children American Sign Language (ASL) and pass on the culture of American deaf people. Deaf teachers and staff also do so, when present; as we shall see, however, deaf adults were increasingly excluded from the schools in the late nineteenth and early twentieth centuries. This process has been going on for nearly two hundred years in America, and for somewhat longer in Europe.[3]

There is a saying that "art imitates life" (*ars imitatur vitam*). I believe the truth is more complex. Sometimes it does, and sometimes it is life that imitates art. In the next chapter I will summarize some of the poignant ways that the public has viewed deaf people over the years. At the same time, as illustrated by the film *The Heart Is a Lonely Hunter*, starring William Hurt and Marlee Matlin, who is deaf in real life, challenged viewers to a different level of understanding and intimacy when Matlin refused to try to use speech and lip reading to communicate with hearing people. In some cases, art truly does imitate life. In other cases, art challenges life to become better by imitating it.

Notes

[1] Harlan Lane, *The Mask of Benevolence: Disabling the Deaf Community* (San Diego, CA: DawnSign Press, 1999), 17.

[2] Gordon Allport, *The Nature of Prejudice* (25th Anniversary Edition Paperback) (New York City: Basic Books, 1979).

[3] Douglas C. Baynton, *Forbidden Signs: American Culture and the Campaign against Sign Language* (Chicago: The University of Chicago Press, 1996), 2.

Chapter 5
Popular Media Portrayals of the Deaf

I wrote the following poem, "Folding Up My Tent," a few days after I suddenly became deaf after routine knee surgery. My whole view of the world was overturned. I was thrust into silence, watching others communicate just by using their lips. The only sounds I heard then were a traffic-like buzz in my right ear and "This Is My Father's World" playing repetitively in my left. I did not know which message to believe, as they seemed to be warring not just over my soul but over my life itself. In despair this poem was born from my desperate and hopeless soul.

Folding up my Tent
Mary Heron Dyer
May 2008

I just finished *Skeletons on the Zahara*,
an account of the shipwreck of American sailors
off the west coast of Africa in 1815.
Within a day they were captured by a wandering tribe of Bedouins,
wending the wind-shifting dunes with their camels.
Life was lived at the edge—
of food, of foliage—
camel urine filling in
when the muddied oases had given up their last drop of moisture,
the contents of the rumen of a newly killed beast
seen as blessed fulfillment of beastly hunger.
And yet,
when the dearly desired and desperately needed night descended,
making it bearable to lie on the cooling sands,
there was always the option of folding up one's tent quietly
and stealing off alone into the silvery night.
What was the tipping point,
where it seemed better to go one's way alone,
to roll the dice carved of camel bone
on the desert floor,
not knowing—or even caring—
if it came up a seven or snake's eyes?
Life or death—
in the flick of a wrist, the blink of an eye.

I wrote this poem because I am deaf, but I am also *not* deaf. While medically deaf and totally immersed in the Deaf experience for more than half a year, I am still basically a hearing person, albeit with no unassisted hearing. Yet I can only visit the land of the hearing, and from time to time my "visa" expires (battery fail, promised assistive listening not in place, etc.). The book *Skeletons on the Zahara* is about a group of American sailors who were shipwrecked on the west coast of Africa in 1815, then immediately captured by a tribe of Bedouins.[1] It is a masterpiece of historical adventure. These shipwrecked sailors were sold into slavery and subjected to a hellish two-month journey through the bone-dry heart of the Sahara. Here they were tested by barbarism, murder, starvation, death, dehydration, and hostile tribes that roamed the desert on camelback. The story records their courage, brotherhood, and survival.

In many ways I am still in a desert and always will be. Before I got my cochlear implant, Sheryl and I, students at Pacific School of Religion in Berkeley, California, got free breakfasts twice a month, paid for by the Disciples of Christ, the denomination into which we would ultimately be ordained. Sheryl usually had to act as my "hearing dog," helping me stay connected to the hearing group, but it was unfair to make her do it all the time. So this one time, after I ordered my blueberry pancakes, conversation just swirled around me, even though I had a pencil and pad right next to me.

As I could see around me the animated faces of fellow seminarians and the faculty staff, I withdrew more and more, wondering why I had even bothered to come. Mostly, to be perfectly honest, it was the free blueberry pancakes! As soon as I finished them, I stood up, faced all of them and said, "I am fucking tired of being ignored," then stomped out of the room to walk down the steep hill to my beginning ASL class. It was one of the highlights of my life. Before I arrived at the classroom, my text messages lit up with several apologies from my hearing companions. This still goes on from time to time, where I am left in the hearing loss desert yet again.

One can see how these two communities—Deaf and LGBT—were formed in adversity and through commonly and tenaciously held misperceptions simply by taking a quick look at classic portrayals of the deaf and homosexuals[2] in films and literature. This list is merely illustrative, not exhaustive.

Johnny Belinda (1948)[3]

This insightful film, starring Lew Ayres and Jane Wyman, offers an inside view of how most hearing people view deaf people. Belinda McDonald is born to a hard-scrabble family of farmers. Being deaf does not save her from backbreaking work on the farm, with long daylight hours. Her parents have no idea of her innate intelligence. Then a new doctor comes to town and takes it upon himself to teach her sign language, which opens the prison doors to her liberation.

The Heart Is a Lonely Hunter (1968)[4]

Twenty years later in 1968, The Heart Is a Lonely Hunter, based on a short story by Carson McCullers, was released, starring Alan Arkin as John Singer, a deaf man who uncomplainingly and selflessly "takes on" perhaps not the sins but certainly the stories of the other characters. Ironically, his deafness becomes a "sounding board" for a teenage girl whose mother owns the boarding house where he lives. He plays this role as well with an angry Black doctor. Yet there is no one to listen to John. Unable to assuage his own loneliness, he commits suicide.

Children of a Lesser God (1986)[5]

In a little less than forty years, we go from the deaf "innocence" of Jane Wyman to the feisty, gutsy, undefeated Marlee Matlin. She plays Sarah Norman, a school janitor, a job she can do silently while being ignored by both faculty and the deaf students. Sarah refuses to try to take a lesser place in the hearing world. She demands that her speech continue to be sign and that her world be valued as much as that of the hearing establishment that has tried so long to deprive her and other students of their history and heritage.

It soon becomes clear why the movie is called *Children of a Lesser God*: deaf children attend a school that aggressively promotes oralism, where, even in the best-case scenario, they will indeed to be children of a "lesser god," born deaf and trying to fit into a hearing world through lip reading and speech lessons. When a new teacher, played by William Hurt, falls in love with Sarah, he insists on her using speech and lip reading. Again, she adamantly refuses.

The following list includes additional films with a leading deaf character.

2000 *Signs of Us*
2001 *Read My Lips*
2002 *Speakeasy*
2004 *It's All Gone Pete Tong*
2004 *Touch the Sound: A Sound Journey with Evelyn Glennie*
2005 *The Quiet*
2007 *Through Deaf Eyes*
2008 TV movie: *Sweet Nothing in My Ear*
2009 *Hear Me*
2009 *See What I'm Saying: The Deaf Entertainers Documentary*
2010 *The Hammer*
2011 *Silenced*

2011 *Planet of Snail*
2011 *Deaf Jam*
2012 *Barfi!*
2012 *The Seasoning House*
2013 *No Ordinary Hero: The Super Deafy Movie*
2013 *Lake Windfall*
2014 *The Belier Family*
2014 *The Tribe*
2015 *The Silent Heroes*
2016 *Dawn of the Deaf*
2017 *Wonderstruck*
2017 *The Silent Child*
2017 *Sign Gene: The First Deaf Superheroes*
2018 *A Quiet Place*
2020 *A Quiet Place Part II*
2019 *The Silent Natural*
2021 *The Djinn*
2021 *Midnight*
2021 *CODA*

The final film on this list is worth exploring further. *CODA*, 2021, is a poignant story about a family in which both the parents and the son are deaf, thus pressuring the hearing daughter, even at an early age, to act as an interlocutor with the hearing world. Her "help" allows the little family to remain very isolated. Yet, as the daughter grows into maturity, she develops a talent for singing. She must decide: will she ultimately go out on her own, or will she be held back by the family she has assisted since she was a small child?

To see how a real, nonfictional family has dealt with such riveting conflicts, a great place start is with the documentaries *Sound and Fury* (2000) and its brief sequel, *Sound and Fury: 6 Years Later* (2006). In these short biographical films, the deaf family fights over whether their deaf daughter, Heather Artinian, might benefit from the advantages of a cochlear implant. When those against the implant win, the entire family decides to move to a culturally separated small community where sign language is the only way to communicate.

But Heather continued to fight to receive cochlear implant surgery and won that right, thus becoming a member of both the hearing and deaf worlds. When her deaf mother realized Heather's growth and transformation, she received a cochlear implant, along with two of her other deaf children. Heather went on to college is now a successful lawyer in a big law firm, with mostly hearing partners.

In all of these films, the themes of "Wholly Other" or "Holy Other" play out in both fiction and biography. It is possible, with a vision, hard work, and commitment, to break the seemingly high and impregnable barrier that separates the two worlds. For instance, in the 2019 biographical film, *The Silent Natural*, set in the 1800s, a deaf ballplayer in the Deaf Major League of Baseball, William Hoy, introduces hand signals for strike and ball to the game and overcomes many obstacles to become one of the greatest players of his time. We see this crossover on national television at sporting events. In baseball, the catcher uses his fingers to signal to the pitcher what to pitch. Hand signals are rife in football and virtually all other sports as well, yet only in writing this book did I find the inspirational story of William Hoy.

Another deaf historical figure who features prominently in creative media is Helen Keller. She was a hearing toddler until measles cruelly took away her hearing (along with her sight). As she grew into adulthood and her parents aged, she probably would have been consigned to a mental hospital for the rest of her natural life. There was no way to communicate with the young child or to educate her until the miraculous intervention of Anne Sullivan, herself the product of a deaf school. Sullivan did have some hearing, but she alone believed in the capacity to overcome her handicap and become a light to the entire world, learning sign language, speech, and lip reading. What a gift would have been wasted if this "Miracle Worker" had not found Helen and become her companion for a much larger life.

In my own life, not knowing if I would ever regain my hearing, I started going to ASL classes in downtown Berkeley, where the teacher and I were the only deaf people in the room. This was actually a delight, as the professor told the class that from that point forward, even at breaks, we could use only sign language to communicate with one another. But of course, that was an artificially constructed, temporary world, not the real one.

The real-world separation was reinforced at a monthly meeting of the People with Disabilities Club at Pacific School of Religion. I was the only deaf person present, though still able to avail myself of the ADA-provided CART interpreter. One day, a classmate, a little person, shared about ways he was discriminated against in public. He was often subject to too-loud whispers about him as he walked by, and he told us he wanted to shout back at them, "I am a little person, but I am not deaf!" At that point, he realized he was standing next to me and turned to apologize.

I tell people that I only have a visa to the hearing world, and it can be revoked at any time. Just recently I lost track of my hearing instrument. After only a brief search, my anxiety reached nuclear proportions, and I started shouting at my hearing spouse, who kept messaging me, "Where did you last see it?" As the seconds turned into minutes and the clock hand kept going forward, I became hysterical, beginning to cry and, well, throw a tantrum.

My whole tentative world of hearing had yet again peremptorily and cruelly been yanked away. I was actually using my captioned phone to connect with customer service to ask how much a replacement hearing instrument would cost (the last one cost more than $10,000 after insurance), when Sheryl dangled the missing earpiece in front of my eyes. The hearing world and the deaf world are truly in separate spheres, and it takes knowledge, patience, perseverance, and compassion, both through films and, as I just exhibited, in real life, to keep trying to bridge the gap. We will see the same pattern in the following chapter about gay characters in films.

Notes

[1] Dean King, *Skeletons on the Zahara* (Little, Brown, and Company, 2004).

[2] The LGBT community no longer uses the term "homosexual," which was coined in the late nineteenth century and traditionally used pejoratively by the psychological and medical establishment and by society at large. I use it here because, before the Stonewall Riots in 1969, it was the commonly accepted term.

[3] Screenplay by Irma von Cube and Allen Vincent, directed by Jean Nelugesco, Warner Bros., 102 minutes, 1948.

[4] Screenplay by Thomas Ryan, directed by Robert Ellis Miller, Warner Bros.-Seven Arts, 123 minutes, 1968.

[5] Based on 1979 play by Mark Medoff, screenplay by Medoff and Hesper Anderson, directed by Randa Haines, Paramount Pictures, 114 minutes, 1986.

Chapter 6
Popular Portrayals of Gays in the Media

There is an intriguing connection with real life and media, particularly in feature films. When I was first "coming out" as gay, I was forty years old, married, with three children still at home. Through months of therapy after I lost my job in a local Catholic church, whose teachings and community had been the bedrock of my life, my therapist kept asking me about my understanding and experience of sexuality. I was incredibly naïve, probably a "gift" from four years in a private girls' Catholic school, where we had to take a senior-year class on marriage. Of course, it was very traditional, and the subjects of sexual pleasure or homosexuality never came up.

My counselor kept pressing me to reexamine my traditional sex life. No, she was not "recruiting" me. She was happily heterosexual, married, with a couple of children. She even loaned me some of her women's music, notably Cris Williamson's album *The Changer and the Changed*. It felt like falling off a cliff, then finding wings I did not know I had. I took the album home and played it loudly repeatedly on my stereo and sang along with Williamson as I did my housework. Gradually, and at first stumblingly, I faced the new reality that confronted me. When I asked my therapist weeks later if Lutheran Family Services would start a counseling group for people like me, she shied away. After all, it was 1986, and the subject of homosexuality was taboo even among counseling services. The DSM-3 still listed it as a psychiatric disorder.[1]

I remember holding hands with my first woman lover while we watched *Desert Hearts* in 1986, a beautiful love story between a young lesbian and an uptight professor who has just left her husband and is in Arizona for a quickie divorce. It was if the entire gay community breathed a sigh of relief. It was the first gay-positive film we had ever seen. At the end of the movie, when the professor takes the train back to her university job, as the two say goodbye, the older woman stretches out her hand, and the younger woman gets onto the train with her. This film broke into the mainstream with tremendous force and success, giving a sensitive and loving, albeit fictional, portrait of two women looking for love and someone to cherish.

Another more memorable event almost a decade later happened when Ellen DeGeneres, for a long time suspected of being a lesbian, "came out" on "The Puppy Episode" of her show *Ellen*. The lesbian community in Corvallis, Oregon, rented a big banquet room in a downtown restaurant to watch this historic show while eating dinner together. This made *Ellen* the first prime-time sitcom to feature a gay leading character.

DeGeneres stoked the fire by referring to herself as "Lebanese" while resisting attempts to clarify her own sexuality. A week before the long-anticipated show aired, she made a well-publicized "coming out" of her own, appearing on the cover of *TIME Magazine* under the headline "Yep, I'm Gay." An estimated 42,000,000 viewers watched the historic, albeit controversial episode on April 30, 1997. Our cheers could probably be heard by puzzled passersby.

I had been "out of the closet" as soon as I figured it out in 1996, leading me to lose my job and support myself through blue-collar jobs such as gardening, landscaping, grading papers, writing homilies for a Catholic homiletic service (a grand irony!), house painting, home health care, and several more. Ellen's brave personal and character "coming out" gave a great many more of us permission and encouragement to embrace our true identities.

The *Diagnostic and Statistical Manual of Mental Disorders*, with which I became intimately acquainted when earning my master's degree at Oregon State University in 1992, had a lot of catching up to do. The 1952 DSM-1, which is the book for counselors and other mental health professionals, listed homosexuality as a sociopathic personality disorder. By 1973, it was no longer listed that way. The latest volume, DSM-5 (2013), lists it as "gender dysphoria," with the counselor needing to assist the person to understand and accept it.

Our graduate class comprised only twenty-one people, five men and sixteen women. I was "out" from the beginning and kept raising concerns and questions about the exclusion of LGBT people in our virtually all of our classes. They were all based exclusively on the heterosexist model. As the first year wore on, four other women "came out" in class after my example, but they were all teachers and could not be "out" when they returned to teaching, or they could be terminated immediately.

More than two decades later, a professor I kept in touch with through Facebook told me that my constant questioning and challenging of the normative and unthinkingly exclusivist "heterosexual" context led to the entire counseling faculty going on a retreat to restructure their curriculum so that it would speak to the issues of gay people. It made my day!

It reminded me of the trip to Palestine when Sheryl and I, along with other seminarians and faculty, stayed for a couple of nights in a convent with guest accommodations. When we found our room, it had three twin beds, equally spaced apart. We went ahead and put two of them together, but every time we returned, the housekeeping nun had pulled them apart again. There are morality police even in the Holy Land!

The portrayals of gay and deaf people in films are also more varied and complex than the heterosexual and hearing boxes they had been shoved into without thought. These films both challenge and invite the viewer to see beyond their binary glasses. Early on, while the deaf usually ended up as objects of melodrama and misplaced pity, homosexuals were used either as comic relief or considered morally evil. The groundbreaking and still definitive book that shed much-needed light on this subject is Vito Russo's *The Celluloid Closet*,[2] first published in 1981 and made into a film in 1996.[3] In the introduction, Russo states,

> In a hundred years of movies, homosexuality has only rarely been depicted on the screen. When it did appear, it was there as something to laugh at—or something to pity—or even something to fear. These were fleeting images, but they were unforgettable, and they left a lasting legacy. Hollywood, that great maker of myths, taught straight people what to think about gay people…and gay people what to think about themselves.[4]

Russo researched the history of how motion pictures, especially Hollywood films, had portrayed gay, lesbian, bisexual, and transgender characters. The film version of his book was initially given a limited release in select theaters, including the Castro Theatre in San Francisco in April 1996, and then shown on the cable channel HBO. The documentary was based on interviews with crew to ask them about their personal experiences with these characters in film. The characters ranged from comical to harmful and distorted stereotypes.

Russo then began meticulously to chart the new course to see how the cinematic perception of the typical gay character was beginning to change into a more varied and sympathetic way. Unfortunately, Russo died in 1990s, well before his project had been completed.

The flamboyantly effeminate man was often introduced into the world of the macho cowboy, such as in *Wanderer of the West*[5] and *The Spoilers*.[6] The master of pantomime, Charlie Chaplain himself, is teased for kissing a boy in *Behind the Screen*.[7] And then there was "Sissy"—Hollywood's first gay stock character. The Sissy made everyone feel more manly or womanly by occupying the space in between. He didn't seem to have a sexuality, so Hollywood allowed him to thrive.[8] He was perceived only subliminally as a homosexual, so as a sexless character he was able to pass the "moral" muster. In film, the Sissy is a male character often depicted as effeminate, often used for comedic or villainous purposes.

Vito Russo's book focused on males because it was the "sissiness" of men not the tomboyishness of women that threatened the cultural myth of male dominance. By and large, even in legal codes, lesbianism was neither considered real nor perceived as a threat to society in the same way that male homosexuality was.

We can see how this plays out in the movie *Morocco* (1930).[9] Marlene Dietrich caused a sensation when she finished a number in a nightclub in the film by kissing a young woman in the audience on the lips. But such freedom would be short-lived.

Powerful forces were already at work. Many groups, mostly women and religious, came together to protest the permissiveness being allowed in newer films. They began lobbying to ban them outright. The movie tycoons fought back with a counter suggestion to label movies according to the acceptability of their content. In general, this compromise was acceptable. Thus, all movies are labeled G, PG, PG-13, R, and NC-17, which indicate age restrictions depending on content. In her article subtitled "Hollywood Codebreakers: Twin Bed Blues," Kristin Hunt explains the motivations behind such codes of conduct in the media. I will focus mostly on the twin bed controversy.[10]

In my earliest memories of black and white TV shows such as *Father Knows Best*, the married husband and wife slept in separate twin beds. Since I was prepubescent, it seemed as if twin beds were the standard sleeping arrangement, both in fiction and in real life. I never realized until my research for this book what how controversial the issue was. Did married couples used to sleep in single beds? In movies and shows from the 1930s and 1940s, they certainly did. Couple after couple click off their lamps and settle into identical but separate beds. This even happened in the *I Love Lucy* show where the stars were actually married in real life. Gradually, over time, the resistance softened. Twin beds came closer together. Then very large queen beds were allowed, as long as the couple was separated by a wide space. Now, it would be strange not to see the reality of life reflected in films.

The main goal was to uphold the sanctity of the home and the institution of marriage. Other related issues such as miscegenation, white slavery, sex hygiene and venereal disease, and even scenes of actual childbirth were never allowed. The heterosexual marriage bed(s) had to be protected at all costs! That, however, wasn't the end of it. Rather than disappearing, homosexual characters morphed. They were harder to find but now had a new identity—as cold-blooded villains. Gloria Holden as *Dracula's Daughter* (1936), Judith Anderson as the ominous Mrs. Danvers in Hitchcock's *Rebecca* (1940), and Peter Lorre as Joel Cairo in *The Maltese Falcon* (1941) began a long line of movie characters in which subtle hints of homosexuality are used to make villains more menacing. "The guys that ran that Code weren't rocket scientists," Jay Presson Allen recalls. "They missed a lot of stuff, and if a director was subtle enough, and clever enough, they got around it." "I don't think the censors at that time realized that this was about gay people," said Arthur Laurents of Hitchcock's film *Rope* (1948), for which Laurents wrote the screenplay based on the true story of gay psychopathic murderers Leopold and Loeb.

While *Rope* star Farley Granger made it clear that the actors knew they were playing gay characters, Laurents thought the censors "didn't have a clue what was and what wasn't. That's how it got by."[11]

Lesbians were not invisible but were pigeonholed and stereotyped. They emerged as tough "bull dykes" behind bars, as in *Caged* (1950), or as neurotics, like Lauren Bacall in *Young Man with a Horn* (1950). These characters served as a warning to force women back into the more traditional roles of wife and mother after World War II, during which they were not only permitted but actually encouraged to join the workforce in such roles as portrayed by Rosie the Riveter. As a side note, my family lived next to a woman who did this during World War II. She went on to become an elementary school teacher. The return of the troops following the war put a sudden end to this mixing of sex roles.

And then came television. There were many experiments with television, but it was not patented by RCA until 1939 and did not enter a large number of American homes until after World War II. *Father Knows Best* began on the radio as a series in 1949 and became a television show in 1954. *The Donna Reed Show* debuted in 1958. The moral code at that time always showed couples in twin beds, at least twelve inches apart, but, as mentioned earlier, that gradually changed.[12]

Otto Preminger was the first one to break the rules with his 1944 film *In the Meantime, Darling*.[13] The director had a terrible fight with the producers over showing an army lieutenant in the same bed as his bride. But the scene made it into the final print. Certainly, by the 1960s, married couples in the movies were allowed to sleep in "cozier" queen beds.

The Hays Code, the official name of the code for motion pictures, was a set of guidelines for the United States film industry that regulated the content of movies from 1930 to 1968. The code was named after Will H. Hays, president of the Motion Picture Producers and Distributors of America (MPPDA) at the time. The code was created in response to public outrage over the perceived immorality of Hollywood films and became mandatory for every Hollywood film in 1934. It was designed to provide what it called "wholesome entertainment," which de facto banned nudity, drug use, and anything considered immoral behavior. The list goes on and explicitly includes homosexuality.

The Hays Code began to lose its standing as society moved on by becoming more liberal and open-minded. In 1968, the Motion Picture Association of America replaced the Hays Code with another rating system that classified movies into different categories based on their content. This year marked a significant shift in the movie industry, with filmmakers gaining more artistic freedom that enabled them to explore complex and controversial topics.

While this development certainly isn't irrelevant, it begins the privatization of entertainment. What once was the shared experience of a large number of people, complete with cartoons, a newsreel, and a double feature, started to shift towards a more personal and individual variety of entertainment in people's homes. Perhaps the most notable early rejection of a strict code for television is Ellen DeGeneres's "coming out" on her show *Ellen*, which I mentioned previously. Code or no code, gay characters could not be driven away in the media, though they were inevitably placed on the sidelines. But when actual sex was suggested, the MPPDA blue-penciled it.

Europe, however, did not share these moral restrictions. In 1961, Great Britain produced *Victim*, with Dirk Bogarde as its first openly gay hero.[14] The plot shows the victim being blackmailed due to his homosexuality. When he is arrested and fearing imprisonment, he chooses suicide in his cell. This film was controversial in Great Britain, but it was banned in America. In the end, Bogarde's character doesn't face any legal consequences or conviction; hes is the victim of blackmail and the legal system's unfair treatment of homosexuals at the time. He does, however, visit judgment on himself by suicide.

The Children's Hour, premiering in the same year, was based on a play by Lillian Hellman starring the well-known actors Shirley MacLaine and Audrey Hepburn.[15] The film dealt with accusations of lesbianism in a girls' school. As in *Victim*, things do not end well for the gay character. Martha, after having admitted her sexual feelings for Karen, hangs herself.

In response to declining revenue, Hollywood realized that audiences were hungry for movies with more "adult" themes and began slowly whittling away at the code put in place in 1930. "Sex perversion," a euphemism for homosexuality, was the last one to go. Otto Preminger forced the issue by announcing, prematurely it turns out, that the code had been revised to allow him to film *Advise and Consent* in 1962, with the subplot concerning a US Senator (played by Don Murray) who is blackmailed about a homosexual affair in his past.[16] Senator Anderson, a Utah Mormon who is trying to block the appointment of a new Secretary of State considered too "dovish" during the Cold War, is blackmailed with a picture that blows his cover as a happily heterosexually married man with children. In a tragic ending similar to that in *Victim* and *The Children's Hour*, he shoots himself in the head to end the disgrace about to be visited upon his family.

Just when it seemed there was no hope for gay characters, Hollywood made a movie in which gay men took a hard look at their own lives and surprisingly, given their fatalistic history in previous films, they all survived. That movie was *Boys in the Band* (1970), based on the hit off-Broadway play by Mart Crowley, and it offered an image of gay men as having a sense of camaraderie.[17] This came on the heels of the Stonewall Uprising, where gay men and women were coming out and claiming their place in society.[18] With the nine main characters not portraying "sissies" or homicidal killers or other deeply disturbed individuals, their sheer number in this movie removed the onus of having only one gay or lesbian character bear one negative stereotype.

Desert Hearts, filmed in Reno, Nevada (1985), and set in 1959, tells the story of a middle-aged university professor awaiting a divorce who unexpectedly finds her true sexual orientation through a relationship with a younger lesbian.[19] It is regarded as one of the first wide release films to present a positive portrayal of lesbian sexuality. For so many of us, it was a big moment of rejoicing. In 1993, a similar film for gay men, especially poignant in the middle of the AIDS crisis, was *Philadelphia* starring Tom Hanks, who won Best Actor at the Academy Awards for his role.[20] It was the first blockbuster movie that dealt both directly and compassionately with AIDS, telling the story of a gay man who lost his job due to prejudice around AIDS and homosexuality. Then in 2005, twelve years later, *Brokeback Mountain* showed a beautiful, intimate portrait of two men, one of whom was heterosexually married, trying to hide their deepening friendship and sexual relationship, which was portrayed as touching, tender, and very erotic.[21] Starring Heath Ledger and Jake Gyllenhaal, with their own breakout roles, it was almost universally well received.

In the first two and a half decades of the twenty-first century, we have been virtually flooded with a wide variety of LGBT films. I have included below an illustrative, not exhaustive, list.

• *A Single Man*, screenplay by Tom Ford and David Scearce from Christopher Isherwood's novel, directed by Ford, Weinstein Company, 100 minutes, 2009. The film follows an English professor returning to his life a year after the death of his lover. As one would expect from Ford, it is a relentlessly stylish affair with indelible performances by Colin Firth and Julianne Moore.

• *The Kids Are All Right*, written by Lisa Cholodenko and Stuart Blumberg, directed by Cholodenko, Focus Features, 107 minutes, 2010. Julianne Moore and Annette Bening play lesbian mothers to two teenagers. Their blissful modern family is rocked when their kids seek out their sperm-donor father, played by Mark Ruffalo. The family unit falls into crisis when his sudden appearance in their lives causes a rift between the two women as well as their kids.

• *Beginners*, written and directed by Mike Mills, Olympus Pictures, 104 minutes, 2010. This sweet film concerns a Los Angeles artist, played by Ewan McGregor, building a relationship with his newly out father (Christopher Plummer) in the last year of the older man's life. *Beginners* earned Plummer an Academy Award for Best Supporting Actor and featuring a talking Jack Russell terrier.

• *Pariah*, written and directed by Dee Rees, Focus Features, 86 minutes. 2011. Rees's gorgeous directorial debut stars Adepero Oduye as Alike, a Brooklyn teenager who comes to terms with her own sexuality and puts the comforts of friends and family at risk as she discovers how to express her identity.

• *Keep the Lights On*, written by Ira Sachs and Mauricio Zacharias, directed by Sachs, Music Box Films, 101 minutes, 2012. Ira Sachs's autobiographical drama packs a hard punch as it follows a filmmaker, Erick, throughout his relationship with a young lawyer, Paul, which begins as a random sexual encounter and implodes following Paul's drug and sex addiction.

• *Blue Is the Warmest Color*, screenplay by Abdellatif Kechiche and Ghalia Lacroix from Jul Maroh's novel, directed by Kechiche, Wild Bunch, 180 minutes, 2013. This film kept its NC-17 rating for explicit, passionate sex scenes between leads Léa Seydoux and Adèle Exarchopoulos, but at its heart it is a movie about youth, art, heartbreak, and the thrill of exploring one's identity.

• *Pride*, written by Stephen Beresford, directed by Matthew Warchus, 20th Century Fox, 120 minutes, 2014. A group of London LGBT activists form a coalition with striking Welsh miners in Margaret Thatcher's United Kingdom. The Golden Globe-nominated screenplay underscores the need, as urgent as ever, for oppressed groups to form relationships and coalitions with others of similar interests and goals.

• *Tangerine*, written by Sean Baker and Chris Bergoch, directed by Baker, Magnolia Pictures, 88 minutes, 2015. Shot on iPhones along Santa Monica Boulevard's unofficial red-light district, the film follows two transgender sex workers and one lovesick cab driver through a particularly eventful Christmas Eve. Director Sean Baker found his leads—two first-time film actors—at the actual donut shop where much of the movie's action takes place.

• *Carol*, screenplay by Phyllis Nagy from Patricia Highsmith's cult novel *The Price of Salt*, directed by Todd Haynes, The Weinstein Company, 119 minutes, 2015. This lush and seductive film follows a young shopgirl named Therese (Rooney Mara) who finds herself charmed by an alluring older woman named Carol (Cate Blanchett). The two set out on a road trip on which they consummate an unspoken passion for each other—one that ultimately brings ruin to Carol's marriage and awakens dark desires within Therese.

- *Viva*, written by Mark O'Halloran, directed by Paddy Breathnach, 100 minutes, 2015. The life of Cuba's *transformistas* is captured in this father-son story about a boy who wants to perform drag and his father, newly released from prison and unable to accept who his son is. The film is beautifully shot with great music and a close look at Havana in all its run-down and colorful glory.

- *Moonlight*, story by Tarell Alvin McCraney, screenplay by Barry Jenkins, directed by Jenkins, A24, 111 minutes, 2016. In the only film on this list to earn an Oscar for Best Picture—and deservedly so—Jenkins explores masculinity and repression in his study of Chiron, a young man coming of age in Miami (played by three different actors at various stages of his life) who grapples with his sexual identity amid his troubled relationship with his crack-addicted mother. Chiron longs to break free of the predetermined path determined by his environment, a journey set into motion by an encounter with one of his male peers.

- *Handsome Devil*, written and directed by John Butler, Icon Film Distribution, 95 minutes, 2016. This charming Irish movie answers the question: "What if John Hughes were Irish and gay?" Misfit Ned struggles at a rugby-obsessed boarding school until a mysterious new kid moves in and an unlikely friendship changes them both. Along the way, viewers watch a rousing performance from Andrew Scott as an inspiring teacher with a secret of his own and a rugby game set to a Rufus Wainwright song.

- *A Fantastic Woman*, written by Sebastián Lelio and Gonzalo Maza, directed by Lelio, Sony Pictures Classics, 104 minutes, 2017. When her older lover, Orlando, dies suddenly, Marina must put her grief on pause as Orlando's ex-wife and family immediately shun her because she is transgender. The winner of the 2017 Oscar for Best Foreign Language film, Lelio's drama features a stirring lead performance from actress Daniela Vega.

- *Call Me by Your Name*, screenplay by James Ivory based on André Aciman's novel, directed by Luca Guadagnino, Sony Pictures Classics, 132 minutes, 2017. In this achingly beautiful gay male romance movie, Timothée Chalamet plays the precocious Elio, a teenager living in Italy who becomes infatuated with an older American student, Oliver (Armie Hammer), who is staying with his family for the summer. What begins as a contentious friendship turns into a full-blown love affair as the two young men spend their idle summer days in the lush Mediterranean landscape.

- *120 BPM (Beats Per Minute)*, written by Robin Campillo and Philippe Mangeot, directed by Campillo, Memento Films, 140 minutes, 2017. Set in the early 1990s, this energetic and emotional drama follows a group of activists in Paris fighting the government and its slow-moving efforts to battle the HIV/AIDS epidemic. While highlighting the dramatic and powerful work from ACT UP, the film also depicts the personal stories of those fighting for their lives, delivering a human and urgent remembrance of the plague that afflicted millions across the globe—and continues today.

• *Can You Ever Forgive Me?* Screenplay by Nicole Holofcener and Jeff Whitty based on Lee Israel's novel, directed by Marielle Heller, Fox Searchlight Pictures,107 minutes, 2018. Melissa McCarthy received an Oscar nomination for her portrayal of Lee Israel, a caustic celebrity biographer who turns to literary forgery when her career stalls. Richard E. Grant is wonderful as her co-conspirator, but it's McCarthy's attempt at romance with Dolly Wells's shy bookstore owner that gives the movie its heart.

• *Love, Simon*, screenplay by Elizabeth Berger and Isaac Aptaker, based on Becky Albertalli's novel *Simon vs. the Homo Sapiens Agenda*, directed by Greg Berlanti, 20th Century Fox, 110 minutes, 2018. If the movie feels a bit like a CW version of an afterschool special, that's no mistake: teen TV super-producer Greg Berlanti makes his feature film directorial debut here. It's as chaste a love story as you're likely to see in the twenty-first century, but the queer kids of the future need their wholesome entertainment too.

• *Rocketman*, written by Lee Hall, directed by Dexter Fletcher, Paramount Pictures, 121 minutes, 2019. An Elton John biopic was never going to be understated, but this glittering jukebox musical full of gay fantasia goes over the top and then keeps going.

• *Fire Island*, screenplay by Joel Kim Booster, directed by Andrew Ahn, Searchlight Pictures, 105 minutes, 2022. This loose adaptation of Jane Austen's *Pride and Prejudice* is set at the titular gay paradise and offers a look at the class divide through a modern gay lens. Bowen Yang, Margaret Cho, Matt Rogers, Conrad Ricamora, and James Scully all get a chance to shine, and we get a rare honest look at gay friendship, flirting, and joy.

The following list includes highlights of 2023 LGBT-related films in alphabetical order.

• *All of Us Strangers*, written and directed by Andrew Haigh, Searchlight Pictures, 105 minutes. Haigh's latest film tells the story of Adam and Harry, two neighbors who fall in love while one is seeing ghosts of his parents. The story along with actors Andrew Scott and Paul Mescal are mesmerizing.

• *Bottoms*, written by Emma Seligman and Rachel Sennot, directed by Seligman, Metro-Goldwyn-Mayer Pictures, 91 minutes. Two lesbians start a fight club as a way to meet other women.

• *Dicks: The Musical*, screenplay by Aaron Jackson and Josh Sharp, based on their off-Broadway musical *Fucking Identical Twins*, A24, 86 minutes. Probably the most extreme gay movie in 2023, the film has musical numbers, Gay God, Megan Thee Stallion, Nathan Lane, incest, and, of course, the Sewer Boys. This musical gained significance due to its combination of vulgar humor, Broadway style musical theater, and an outrageous plot. It is both offensive and delightful, both pushing boundaries and providing a wildly entertaining experience.

• *Blue Jean*, written and directed by Georgia Oakley, Attitude Films, 97 minutes. In British writer/director Oakley's debut film, a high school gym teacher named Jean (played by Rosy McEwen) lives in 1980s England when the Conservative party, led by Margaret Thatcher, announces Section 28, which prohibits the "promotion" of homosexuality as a "pretended family relationship." This new law means that if Jean is discovered, she'll be fired from her teaching position. McEwan received rave reviews for her powerful performance as a woman in an impossible situation.

• *Cassandro*, written by Roger Ross Williams and David Teague, directed by Williams, Amazon MGM Studios, 107 minutes. Gael García Bernal brings the story of real-life gay Mexican wrestler Saúl Armendáriz to the screen, shining in a strong and sensitive performance. The entire cast, including Roberta Colindrez and Bad Bunny, is terrific.

• *Every Body*, directed by Julie Cohen, Focus Features, 92 minutes. Cohen's documentary shines a light on part of the LGBTQ+ community that is often overlooked: intersex people. By following three intersex activists—Sean Saifa Wall, Alicia Roth Weigel, and River Gallo—the poignant and personal film allows us to see what life is like for different people in the same community.

• *Knock at the Cabin*, screenplay by M. Night Shyamalan, Steve Desmond, and Michael Sherman, based on *The Cabin at the End of the World* by Paul G. Tremblay, directed by Shyamalan, Universal Pictures, 100 minutes. Ben Aldridge and Jonathan Groff star as two gay dads who travel to a cabin with their daughter for rest and relaxation. Unfortunately, when they get there, they're confronted by a group of attackers led by Dave Bautista (in a terrifically chilling performance) who say that one member of their family must die in order to save the world. It's one of Shyamalan's best in years and features great acting from the whole cast at the cabin.

- *Komoko City*, directed by D. Smith directed, Magnolia Pictures, 73 minutes. Smith also produced and edited this unflinching look at the lives of four Black trans sex workers living in New York and Georgia. The documentary gives a voice to people who are often silenced.

- *M3GAN*, screenplay by Akela Cooper from a story by her and James Wan, directed by Gerard Johnstone, Universal Pictures, 102 minutes. A new horror icon is born when M3GAN, a doll with a killer AI, dances her way onto the screen. This film is scary, campy, and focuses on the chosen family between a woman (played by Allison Williams), her eight-year-old niece Cady, and the intelligent and deadly doll who co-parents the child. The central plot of adoption resonated with the gay and lesbian community because of the idea of a found, not a birth, family.

- *Monica*, written by Andrea Pallaoro and Orlando Tirado, directed by Pallaoro, IFC Films, 106 minutes. Trace Lysette shines in this understated family drama. She plays Monica, a trans woman who returns home to help take care of her ailing mother (Patricia Clarkson), who had kicked her out for transitioning years ago. Lysette's undeniably powerful and understated performance is one of the best from 2023.

- *Mutt*, written and directed by Vuk Lungulov-Klotz, Strand Releasing, 87 minutes. Lío Mehiel had their breakout role in this film, becoming the first out trans actor to win the Sundance Dramatic Special Jury Award for Best Acting. In the movie, they play a trans man named Feña who reconnects with his family and former friends for the first time after his transition.

- *Nimona*, screenplay by Robert L. Baird and Lloyd Taylor, based on *Nimona* by ND Stevenson, directed by Nick Bruno and Troy Quane, Netflix, 99 minutes. Perhaps the best queer film of 2023, this animated movie is about a shapeshifting teen girl and the gay supervillain she befriends. *Nimona* provides fun, action, and comedy but also reveals one of the most powerful messages about love of any movie in recent memory.

- *Nyad*, screenplay by Julia Cox, based on *Find a Way* by Diana Nyad, directed by Elizabeth Chai Vasarhelyi and Jimmy Chin, Netflix, 120 minutes. This biopic stars Annette Bening and Jodie Foster. Bening plays open-water swimmer Diana Nyad, who became the first person to swim from Cuba to Florida without aid at age sixty-four. Both Bening and Foster deliver award-worthy performances. Nyad's friend and former lover, played by Jodie Foster, becomes her coach in this intimate portrait of a continuing deep friendship.

- *Of an Age*, written and directed by Goran Stolevski, Roadshow Films, 100 minutes. This tender gay drama is set in Australia in the summer of 1999. It follows a Serbian teen boy who moves to Australia, becomes an amateur ballroom dancer, and has an unexpected and intense affair with his friend's older brother.

- *Passages*, written by Mauricio Zacharias, Ira Sachs, and Arlette Langman, directed by Sachs, SBS Productions, 92 minutes. This sexy romantic drama stars Ben Wishaw and Franz Rogowski as a gay couple whose marriage endures conflict when one of them begins an affair with a young woman (Adèle Exarchopoulos).

- *Red, White, and Royal Blue*, screenplay by Matthew López and Ted Malawer, based on the book by Casey McQuiston, Amazon Prime Video, 118 minutes. In this modern gay rom-com classic, Taylor Zakhar Perez and Nicholas Galitzine are the sons of the US President and a British Prince who fall in love.

- *Rustin*, screenplay by Julian Breece and Dustin Lance Black, directed by George C. Wolfe, Higher Ground (Netflix), 106 minutes. Colman Domingo plays gay Civil Rights icon Bayard Rustin, delivering an Oscar-worthy performance in this wonderful biopic about queer and Black history.

- *Scream VI*, written by James Vanderbilt and Guy Busick, directed by Matt Bettinelli-Olpin and Tyler Gillett, Paramount Pictures, 122 minutes. The two most recent *Scream* movies have revitalized the franchise with a new group that includes the series' first out queer character, Mindy Meeks-Martin, played by out actor Jasmin Savoy Brown.

- *Monica*, written by Andrea Pallaoro and Orlando Tirado, directed by Pallaoro, IFC Films, 106 minutes. Trace Lysette shines in this understated family drama, playing Monica, a trans woman who returns home to help take care of her ailing mother (Patricia Clarkson) who had kicked her our years earlier for transitioning.

- *Strange Way of Life*, written and directed by Pedro Almodóvar, Saint Laurent Productions, 31 minutes. This short, stylish Western follows Ethan Hawke and Pedro Pascal, fully decked out in Saint Laurent as two aging gunslingers with a romantic past who reunite one last time.

- *Theater Camp*, written by Noah Galvin et al., directed by Molly Gordon and Nick Lieberman, Searchlight Pictures, 93 minutes. This mockumentary-style comedy follows Amos and Rebecca-Diane as they write a musical at a summer theater camp in danger of shutting down when the owner goes into a coma and her son Troy must take over. This movie embraced the LGBTQ+ community by providing positive queer representation for gender expressions. The movie shows gender-non-conforming people, a gay man, and a drag queen, all positively portrayed.

• *The Stroll*, documentary directed by Kristen Lovell and Zackary Drucker, HBO, 84 minutes. The history of New York's meatpacking district is told from the perspective of transgender sex workers who lived and worked there.

Given this extensive list of films, I believe that we have achieved parity with the heterosexual film world. It seems as if there is something for everyone!

As an addendum, I had the recent privilege of watching *Will & Harper*, a 2024 documentary directed by Josh Greenbaum for Netflix (114 minutes). The film is based on a cross-country trip taken by the well-known actor Will Ferrell, most of whose roles are comedic, with a long-term friend from the film industry. Formerly Alan Steele, Harper Steele had just informed her friend Will that she is transgender. Will and Harper did not know how or if that would impact their friendship, so they agreed to take a cross-country road trip to process this new stage of their relationship. The result is an honest, intimate portrait of friendship and transition.

Notes

[1] *Diagnostic and Statistical Manual of Mental Disorders*, 3rd ed. (American Psychiatric Association, 1980), commonly referred to as DSM-3.

[2] Vito Russo, *The Celluloid Closet* (New York: Harper and Row, 1981).

[3] *The Celluloid Closet*, written by Vito Russo et al., directed by Rob Epstein and Jeffrey Friedman, Channel 4 and Home Box Office, 107 minutes, 1996.

[4] Russo, *Celluloid Closet* (book).

[5] *A Wanderer of the West*, silent film, written by A. Hoerl, W. R. Johnston, and V. Rousseau, directed by Robin Williamson and Joseph Zivelli, Trem Carr Pictures, 60 minutes, 1927.

[6] *The Spoilers*, screenplay by Lawrence Hazard and Tom Reed, directed by Ray Enright, Universal Pictures, 87 minutes, 1942.

[7] *Behind the Screen*, silent film, written by Charlie Chaplin, Vincent Bryan, and Maverick Terrell, directed by Chaplin, Mutual Film Corporation, 23 minutes, 1916.

[8] Well-known examples of the Sissy include Pangborn in *My Man Godfrey* and the Cowardly Lion in *The Wizard of Oz*, as well as villainous characters like Buffalo Bill in *Silence of the Lambs* or Waldo Lydecker in *Laura*.

[9] *Morocco*, screenplay adapted by Jules Furthman from Benno Vigny's novel *Amy Jolly*, directed by Josef von Sternberg, Paramount Publix Corporation, 91 minutes, 1930.

[10] Kristin Hunt, "Hollywood Codebreakers: Twin Bed Blues," *Medium*, June 22, 2018 https://medium.com/@kristinhunt/hollywood-codebreakers-twin-bed-blues-57c6c57b6278.

[11] Quotes from Stephen Tropiano, *The Prime-Time Closet: A History of Gays and Lesbians on TV* (New York: Applause Theatre and Cinema Books, 2002).

[12] Hunt, "Hollywood Codebreakers: Twin Bed Blues."

[13] *In the Meantime, Darling*, written by Arthur Kober and Michael Uris, directed by Otto Preminger, 20th Century Fox, 72 minutes, 1944.

[14] *Victim*, screenplay by Janet Green and John McCormick, directed by Basil Dearden, Allied Film Makers and Parkway Films, 100 minutes, 1961.

[15] *The Children's Hour*, screenplay adapted by John Michael Hayes and Lillian Hellman, directed by William Wyler, United Artists, 107 minutes, 1961.

[16] *Advise and Consent*, screenplay by Wendell Mayes based on the novel by Allen Drury, directed by Otto Preminger, Columbia Pictures, 138 minutes, 1962.

[17] *Boys in the Band*, screenplay by Mart Crowley (based on his play), directed by William Friedkin, National General Pictures, 120 minutes, 1970.

[18] See "1969: The Stonewall Uprising," *Library of Congress*, https://guides.loc.gov/lgbtq-studies/stonewall-era.

[19] *Desert Hearts*, screenplay by Natalie Cooper (based on *Desert of the Heart* by Jane Rule), directed by Donna Deitch, Samuel Goldwyn Company, 96 minutes, 1985.

[20] *Philadelphia*, written by Ron Nyswaner, directed by Jonathan Demme, TriStar Pictures, 126 minutes, 1993.

[21] *Brokeback Mountain*, screenplay by Larry McMurtry and Diana Ossana (based on the book by Annie Proulx), directed by Ang Lee, Focus Features, 134 minutes, 2005.

Chapter 7
A Brief History of the Deaf Community in the US before "The Revolution"

I think my favorite film featuring a deaf character is *Children of a Lesser God* (1976). The character, played by Marlee Matlin, who is totally deaf, is forced to learn to speak and to read lips to better fit into the hearing world (i.e., the "normal"). This practice began because of Alexander Graham Bell, who insisted on total oralism for his deaf mother and wife. It became mandatory at the Second International Congress on Education of the Deaf held in Milan in 1880. Yet again, hearing people decided not if but how deaf people needed to give up their culture and language in the hopes that they, like Helen Keller, would "pass" in the hearing world. (Ironically, Keller was born in 1880, the same year the congress laid out its edicts for the deaf.) Is it any wonder that a slogan of the disability movement is "Nothing about us without us."

We have had to deal with this every day in our hearing loop business. When I became deaf, even after I received a cochlear implant, my ability to hear clearly in larger venues or when more than one person was talking was curtailed severely due to the limitations of my artificial hearing. One day I accidentally learned about the not-yet-utilized telecoil in my hearing instrument when the speaker told us that the room had a hearing loop. Fortunately, the meeting was open captioned, as a number of deaf people were there. So I fiddled with my hearing instrument until I found the telecoil setting. Suddenly, it felt as if the speaker was right in my ear, and I could hear clearly for the first time since I had become deaf. After riding home, I burst into our student apartment at the seminary to tell Sheryl. With a divine sense of irony, we learned what hearing loops were, how to install them, and became instant advocates and educators for people with hearing loss. Once we had learned the essentials, we went to the IT team at the seminary and showed them how hearing loops worked, and soon our student chapel installed one, as required by the ADA.

Sheryl was doing her student chaplaincy on the same day as our weekly chapel, so she was surprised when she got back and found me sitting in the front pew all the way to the left, near the audio room. The IT team did not know they could extend the hearing loop wire into the pews, so I was sitting literally in the only seat in the chapel that could access the sound.

My sudden deafness led to our entire ministry once Sheryl was ordained, so we began Hearing Access Solutions, whose sole mission was to do education and advocacy around hearing loss and to install hearing loops. So far, we have installed hundreds of hearing loops all over the Midwest, with the largest business coming from houses of worship.[1]

My personal experience with totally deaf people came when the previous governor of Iowa appointed me to the Iowa Deaf Services Commission. I served from 2015 to 2019. Sometimes I was the only person with hearing loss there, as opposed to several members who were born deaf. It was like a hearing loss United Nations meeting, with participants speaking in several different languages. There was always an ASL interpreter, captioning, and speaking. I could usually hear well enough not to need the captioning, but it was a good backup. When a deaf member signed, I had to look at the ASL interpreter for them to speak it out loud, which was also captioned. Even the deaf members who could speak clearly chose not to. When it was lunchtime, we all went out. I wanted to sit with the deaf members, but it seemed to be a "members only" club. It actually reminded me of how the gay community was in the eighties. We were very protective of ourselves, since our exclusion seemed to be intransigent. It was not until our Walk Against Hate in 1992 that we discovered, much to our surprise, that there were a great many people and institutions that welcomed us, fed us, housed us, and heard our stories.

The Deaf Revolution (also known as "Deaf President Now"; see chapter 12) was the keystone of similar revolutions to follow. It started in 1988, when students at Gallaudet University, the only university in the world at that time designed to be barrier-free for deaf and hard-of-hearing students, seized control of their campus through nonviolent actions. They took up a collection, bought locks, and chained the gates to the campus shut. They marched. They campaigned. They refused to relent until the Board of Trustees granted their core demand: appoint a deaf president to lead Gallaudet. There were three candidates for the position, all well qualified. Two were deaf, so they had a lived experience of the Deaf community. One was hearing. The board initially chose the hearing woman over the two capable deaf candidates.

A week after the protests began, the board appointed Dr. I. King Jordan as president. Jordan quickly became a global leader for deaf and disability rights. The power demonstrated by the Gallaudet students fueled efforts around deaf rights for years to come (including later protests at Gallaudet) and also helped catalyze efforts to pass the Americans with Disabilities Act (1990). The lessons from Deaf President Now should be clear. Its success, fueled by direct action, shows that rights have to be claimed rather than given. This series of protests stands as a watershed moment in the history not only of deaf and disability rights but also all other American civil rights.

The Americans with Disabilities Act (ADA) of 1990 is a civil rights law that prohibits discrimination against individuals with disabilities in various aspects of public life. It aims to ensure that people with disabilities have the same opportunities as everyone else in areas like employment, education, transportation, and access to public accommodations. The ADA was signed into law on July 26, 1990.[2] We have learned the hard way that it is easier said or written, rather than done, but being able to cite the specific provisions of the ADA that apply to those with hearing loss has made most colleges and universities comply with ways to assist people who fit that category. The battle, however, is not yet over.

How did hearing people come to be the ones who make decisions on how deaf people are supposed to live their lives? Reducing such a complex subject to a few paragraphs is a foolish task. Even so, at least a brief overview of these two minority communities of both the Deaf and LGBTQ is essential before moving forward.

Let us start with the deaf, who have a long history of their struggles. Socrates, Aristotle, and St. Augustine studied their problems, but only in the sixteenth century were any real efforts made to teach the deaf.[3] Spanish monk Pablo Ponce de Leon, a Benedictine monk living in San Salvador, met a man who had been refused as a member of the community because of his deafness. De Leon taught this man to read and speak well enough to be accepted as a postulant. Years later, De Leon established a school north of Madrid where he tutored the deaf children of rich parents. In 1620, the first book on educating deaf children was written by Juan Pablo Bonet, also a Spaniard, who advocated both manual communication and speech. Translated, its title is *Summary of the letters and the art of teaching speech to the mute*. From the early 1600s to 1755, deaf students were generally educated using a combination of speech instruction along with some form of manual communication.

The situation changed radically when Abbe Charles-Michel de l'Épée (1712–1789) founded the world's first public school for deaf children. While he did not specifically condemn the teaching of speech and speech reading, he did not emphasize it. Under him and his successor, Abbe Roch-Ambroise Cucurron Sicard (1742–1822), the use of sign language gradually supplanted almost all use of speech.

At this point, we can begin to cobble together the history of the deaf in the United States. It begins with the extraordinary life of Thomas Hopkins Gallaudet (1787–1851), a young seminarian interested in deaf education. This interest led to his eventually meeting Alice, his private pupil with whom he communicated in sign. The two later married. As his interest in the deaf expanded, Gallaudet first went to Great Britain to observe the teaching methods of the oralist school founded by the Brainwoods in 1760. Rebuffed by them, since they held their methods proprietarily, he then went to France, where he was warmly welcomed at the Royal School for Deaf-Mutes and saw the obvious successes of sign language.

Convincing a deaf student, Laurent Clerc, to return to the States with him to teach, Gallaudet opened the first school for the deaf in Hartford, Connecticut, in 1817, a school placed firmly in the signing camp. One of his eight children, Thomas Miner Gallaudet, took over his father's mantle, continuing to preach signing as a primary method to be implemented with the oral method as needed and appropriate. At the same time, the oralist camp was gaining adherents in the United States. By the 1860s, oral schools like the New York Institution for the Improved Instruction of Deaf-Mutes and the Clarke Institution for Deaf-mutes in Northampton, Massachusetts, were established.

And then came Alexander Graham Bell. Both his experience at home and at the Clarke Institution made him a firm, increasingly doctrinaire adherent of oralism as the *only* method for instructing the deaf. Bell's mother, Eliza Bell, had lost most of her hearing as a child but had strong speech and language skills. She used an ear trumpet for communication, while her husband, Melville Bell, developed Visible Speech to teach hearing people proper elocution. He also believed that this system could be used to teach profoundly deaf people to speak intelligibly. When Alexander Graham Bell married Mabel Hubbard, who had lost her hearing around the age of five but who, like Eliza, retained excellent language skills, his fate was sealed. He was entrenched in the oralist camp. Both his mother and wife refused to use any sign or even to be seen in public with other deaf people.

The tremendous impact of this wholehearted, albeit unthinking embrace of oralism, to the exclusion of manualism, on the Deaf community cannot be overstated. In an article by Charlotte Baker and Robbin Battison, the authors state,

> Mouthing and the use of speech represent many things to Deaf people. Since speech has traditionally been forced on Deaf people as a substitute for their language, it has come to represent confinement and denial of the most fundamental need of Deaf people: to communicate deeply and comfortably in their own language. Deaf people often distrust speech communication for this reason. In speaking, the Deaf person feels she will always be at a disadvantage and can never become fully equal to hearing people who, from the viewpoint of the Deaf person, are always the more accurate models of speaking.[4]

Albert Ballin states the point even more strongly in *The Deaf-Mute Howls*. Ballin, who was deaf, was born in 1861 to a deaf father, a lithographer who had emigrated from Germany at the age of twenty-two. Ballin mastered several languages as well as speaking and lip-reading, and he wrote not only for the deaf press but also for other magazines and newspapers. While eschewing oralism, going head-to-head with Bell, Ballin had a much more far-reaching solution. He proposed to disband deaf residential schools and challenged head-on the hearing world's consistently hegemonic assumptions towards *all* disabled people:

> Oralism was the remedy offered by hearing people. Let all deaf people learn to speak and lip-read and the gulf between deaf and hearing people would be bridged. This of course is what hearing people tend always to ask from deaf people, what nondisabled people have always wanted from disabled people, and indeed what majorities have always wanted from minorities—that they adjust, change, make the effort, surmount the barriers. If deaf people would just learn to converse with hearing people in the manner to which hearing people are accustomed, then the deaf community would be "restored to society."[5]

Joseph Schuyler Long, a contemporary of Ballin, wrote in 1890 that "Chinese women bind their babies' feet to make them small; the Flathead Indians bind their babies' heads to make them flat. And the people who prevent the sign language being used in the education of the deaf…are in the same class of criminals."[6] This brief history, as exemplified by the intransigent stance between Bell and Gallaudet, shows the clear battle lines drawn by the end of the nineteenth century.

Other dates and events are important, such as the Conference of Milan in 1880, which came down firmly in the oralist camp and almost eradicated deaf language and culture as waves of oralism swept the world. Then, in 1901 the first electric hearing aid (radio aid) was developed, ultimately leading to the debate surrounding cochlear implants. Cochlear implants could be used for many deaf children, but in general, if the child's parents were deaf, they fought hard against giving the child access to hearing, fearing that the child would enter the hearing world and leave them behind. Oralism kept its stranglehold on deaf education for almost a hundred years, with sign being passed on in secret among deaf children in their dormitories at oralist schools.

Before World War II, the Deaf community was relatively self-contained. Most major cities had deaf clubs where the Deaf would congregate for socializing, networking, and giving one another support. The entertainment industry, especially with the demise of silent films and the advent of "talkies," meant that the deaf were de facto excluded from movies, plays, musicals, and more, so they continued to rely on their own devices for dances and performances, developing deaf stories, humor, and a subculture to hand down their stories and history.

World War II was a pivotal turning point at the beginning of a wider inclusion of the deaf in the larger community. Because of the work shortage created by the military's need for millions of men, wide gaps appeared in the stateside labor force. Until that time, the Deaf community largely worked either in trades, where they could be independent and self-supporting, or in industries such as printing and linotype or woodworking for the men and sweatshops for the women. With the job vacancies occurring as men were drafted, both the deaf and women were eagerly recruited for industries supplying the war machine. Here they proved both competent and loyal, with the side effect of successfully challenging and ultimately changing many stereotypes about their capacity and reliability.

After the war, many deaf people were able to retain their jobs in heretofore exclusionary industries. They had proved their mettle during trying national times and earned a place at the table—or, one should say, at *some* tables. It would take the Americans with Disabilities Act of 1990 to set the table for further advances. This act delineates in detail the provisions an employer must make to accommodate a worker with a disability, if such accommodation would allow that worker to perform the job satisfactorily. This applies not only to physical access but also to communications.

While it gained broad bipartisan support for passage, some groups and individuals raised concerns about the ADA's impact on their interests. Small businesses expressed concerns about the financial burden of compliance, fearing lawsuits and the cost of making buildings and facilities accessible while others questioned the broad definition of "disability." Many religious groups also raised loud complaints. For instance, the Association of Christian Schools International and the National Association of Evangelicals initially opposed the ADA, particularly its labeling of religious institutions as "public accommodations." They argued that this would require churches to make costly structural changes and potentially violate religious liberty. Their fear was unfounded, since the ADA exempts all facilities, programs, and activities of religious programs. Ironically, though, most of our hearing loop installs are in churches. Sometimes guilt is the motive, especially when many churches display an "All Are Welcome" sign in front of their buildings and on their websites.

Advances in technology, particularly those that would enhance the communication of the deaf, assisted them in widening their horizons on one hand while making the flourishing and ultimately even the existence of deaf subculture moribund on the other. For example, technology such as the TTY (telephone typewriter) or TDD (telecommunications device for the deaf) was invented in 1964. This electronic device allowed text communication via a telephone line and was used when one or more of the parties had hearing or speech difficulties. It enabled the deaf to use telephones to communicate not only with one another but also with the hearing world, as computers and the concomitant capacity of the Web broke down barriers of geography and language. Deaf people gradually found a place in a much larger world than they would have dreamed of before World War II and the technology and communications advancements that followed it.

Now there are telephones available to the deaf and to the hard-of-hearing who can speak that are captioned for them when they converse with a hearing person. There are also phones with video relays, which allow those who communicate in sign rather than speech to do real-time, long-distance conversations in sign. While these are wonderful advances, they do mean that there is a concomitant lesser dependence on other deaf people, particularly in deaf clubs and social networks, because of the ability to communicate in these more inclusive ways.

It is intriguing that this divide of deaf people and LGBTQ+ people existed until the barriers began to come down in the last several decades of the twentieth century. For the Deaf community, the Gallaudet Deaf Revolution at the university was the dividing line. For the first time in the history of the United States, they were able to force the board to elect a deaf candidate rather than the hearing professor first elected. In retrospect, it seems natural and fitting that this should have happened before, but it was the student walkout that forced the board's hand and raised their awareness of this seemingly obvious inequity. It reminds me of the rallying cry for the disability rights movement in the 1990s, originally popularized by South African disability rights activists. Now most people understand that colonial superiority subordinated minority populations of any kind over the centuries, be it Native Americans, former slaves, the disabled, women, and others.

With the issue of gay rights, it has always been a "moral" matter whereby ignorant people, using the Bible as a weapon and unwilling to accept that gender is fluid, continue both their prejudice and growing attempts to reverse the rights we have already gained. Foremost, of course, is our own right to marry. My spouse Sheryl and I made our first commitment on May 1, 2005, in front of our two Italian greyhounds and kitten. We never kept our relationship secret, but still I could not be added to her health insurance or have a natural right of power of attorney, visitation in a hospital, church membership, and ordination. The list goes on and on.

It has been largely a moral revolution in which we are still fighting to be not grudgingly accepted but welcomed with all of our unique gifts. Virtually all the mainstream churches now support full membership and ordination of LGBTQ+ people , including the church where my spouse Sheryl and I have full clerical standing, the Christian Church (Disciples of Christ). A dear friend of ours from our Pacific School of Religion days, Karen Oliveto, became the first openly gay bishop in the United Methodist Church. Even then, it was a wedge issue that split the Methodists into two separate groups, and they are no longer legally connected.

Bishop Oliveto showed great courage and grace at the forefront of social and religious change while she was simultaneously commended and condemned.[7]

Herodotus, the fifth century BCE Greek historian and geographer, claimed that "No man ever steps in the same river twice." The currents swirl and the water moves, sometimes lazily, sometimes in a rush, inevitably to its outlet, where it joins other rivers flowing into the sea. Thus are the currents of mercy and justice, overcoming obstacles, dashing against rocks, and finding new channels, but they keep rolling along.

Notes

[1] For more, see Hearing Access Solutions LLC at www.hasloops.com.

[2] See https://www.ada.gov/law-and-regs/ada/.

[3] Richard Winefield, *Never the Twain Shall Meet: Bell, Gallaudet, and the Communications Debate* (Washington, DC: Gallaudet University, 1987).

[4] Charlotte Baker and Robbin Battison, "The deaf community and the culture of deaf people," in *Sign Language and the Deaf Community*, ed. Carol Padden (Silver Spring, MD: National Association of the Deaf, 1980), cited in Jerome E. Schein, *At Home among Strangers: Exploring the Deaf Community in the United States* (Washington, DC: Gallaudet University Press, 1989), 33.

[5] Albert Ballin, *The Deaf-Mute Howls* (Washington, DC: Gallaudet University Press, 1998), xxviii.

[6] Ibid., xvi.

[7] For more, see Karen Oliveto's book, *Our Strangely Warmed Hearts*.

Chapter 8
LGBT History in the United States before Stonewall in 1969

As I edited this manuscript, I noticed a glaring omission. I was born in November 1945, right after World War II had ended. Both of my parents were WWII veterans…and Republicans. Patriotism was woven into my young life. I vaguely remember the McCarthy witch hunts. I would proudly stand up, place my hand over my heart, and recite "The Pledge of Allegiance" with my young classmates at the drop of a hat. In my young adult life, especially after having a front-row seat to the police riots at University of California Santa Barbara where I was a student in the late sixties and early seventies, as a counterforce to the largely peaceful student protests against the Vietnam War, I took a vow never to recite the pledge again. I viscerally knew that "with liberty and justice for all" were idle and largely untrue words. One of my fondest memories was being part of a peace march beginning at the Santa Barbara Mission and moving down to the harbor.

Years later, I went with my daughter and grandchildren to a local baseball game that started with the usual patriotic display. When I did not stand with the others while it was going on, my teenaged granddaughter asked me why. I explained that I would not stand for a pro forma show of patriotism. Most people who follow football remember what happened to Colin Kaepernick when he refused to stand at attention to the flag at an NFL football game but knelt instead in order to protest racial inequality and police brutality. It was as if the sky had fallen in, and he is still living with the results.

Like other minority communities, the LGBT community has won many fights, but as the saying goes, "The price of liberty is eternal vigilance." For the past few years, we have experienced an upsurge of hatred of LGBT people and legislation drafted against them in almost every state in this country. It even became one of the third rails of the 2024 election. Just as lack of attention and foresight contributed to the 1973 *Roe v. Wade* SCOTUS decision being overturned in 2022, these two third-rail issues, the place and rights of both LGBT people and *all* females, are yet again being challenged.

So let us start with the possibility of another gender identity, where our gender-fluid identities emerged under the pen of Sappho, a woman-loving woman born two and a half millennia ago on the small Greek island of Samos.

Lavender and the LGBT Community

Why is lavender associated with the LGBT community? It all began on the Greek island of Samos more than two and a half millennia ago. Sappho, a poet known all over the western world, lived there with a cohort of other women. From lavender to violets, purple flowers have an undeniable lesbian legacy. They crop up repeatedly in lesbian iconography throughout history, with each instance building on those that came before.

The first evidence of this phenomenon occurred in the sixth century BCE poetry of Sappho, fabled to be the first known woman-loving woman. Her significance cannot be overstated; her influence is so profound that the word "lesbian" is derived from Lesbos, the island where she lived and wrote. From "Sappho" came the word "sapphic" to refer to any woman-loving woman (WLW).

Although, sadly, only fragments of Sappho's ancient poetry remain, historians and literary critics note myriad references to flowers—especially purple blooms. Her surviving work conjures images of idyllic pastures where girls and women frolic, adorned in beautiful plumage, as the poem "Many crowns of violets" shows:

> Many crowns of violets,
> roses and crocuses…
> together you set before more
> and many scented wreaths
> made from blossoms
> around your soft throat…
> …with pure, sweet oil
> …you anointed me,
> and on a soft, gentle bed…
> you quenched your desire…
> …no holy site…
> we left uncovered, no grove...

Her poem "For Willyce" is a bit more graphic:

> When I make love to you
> I try
> With each stroke of my tongue
> to say   I love you
> to tease   I love you
> to hammer   I move you
> to melt.   I love you
>
> & your sounds drift down
> Oh god!
> And I think—
> Here it is, some dude's

Getting credit for what
A woman
Has done,
Again.

Sappho must have imagined that her poems would be discovered and even memorialized millennia later. She stated, "You may forget but let me tell you this: someone in some future time will think of us." I expect she would be pleased and honored by her influence on the gay movement.

Later, during the time of the Roman Empire, the color purple was associated with power, prestige, and imperial authority. It was more than a visual delight—it was a potent symbol of status and influence. Its historical significance in Roman society reveals why this vibrant hue became the color of emperors and gods. It was not until much later that it became possible to create this color inexpensively, which is another reason it was originally reserved for emperors and gods.

In addition, the sumptuary laws were legislated as early as 215 BCE. The Sumptuariae Leges of ancient Rome were various laws passed to prevent inordinate expense (Latin "sumptus") in banquets and dress, such as the use of expensive Tyrian purple dye. Roman senators and senior magistrates were entitled to wear a Tyrian purple stripe on their togas and tunics. The law was designed to restrict excessive personal expenditures in the interest of limiting extravagance and luxury to only a few. The term denotes regulations restricting extravagance in food, drink, dress, and household equipment, usually on religious or moral grounds. Such laws proved difficult or impossible to enforce over the long term.

Strangely enough, the color purple is even mentioned in the New Testament in the story of Lydia, a purple-dye maker. She was a convert to Christianity. Lydia is mentioned only a few times in the New Testament, in Acts 16:11-15, 40. Though purple dye can be made from the madder plant, the only true purple colorfast dye known at that time was produced by the murex snail, a marine mollusk. Debates continue as to whether Lydia used the madder plant or the murex, but either way, making purple dye was a difficult, costly, and time-consuming process. As a result, purple dye was purchased by royalty, elites, and the very wealthy, who used it to have a border of purple on the hems of their garments, like the senators in Rome on their togas.

In early twentieth-century Paris, violets were once again taken on as a purposeful lesbian adornment among a group dubbed "Paris Lesbos." The group of women included Renée Vivien, a British poet who started a new life in Paris. Violets were a motif both in her poetry and in her personal style. This can partly be read as homage to Sappho, but it was also honoring Renée's first love, Violet Shillito.

Fellow author Colette recalled that "whenever she gave me any of her books, she always hid them under a bouquet of violets or a basket of fruit."

Decades later, in Édouard Bourdet's 1926 play *The Captive*, one female character sends bunches of violets to another female character. The semi-public association with lesbianism caused an uproar, leading to calls for boycott and censorship of the play. At some showings in Paris, women wore violets on their lapels as signs of support. After production was eventually shut down in 1927, the negative connotations caused plummeting violet sales in the USA—to the extent that seven years later, florists were still feeling the effects. Historian, writer, and lecturer Eleanor Medhurst, in her book *Unsuitable: A History of Lesbian Fashion* (2024), is said to have remarked, "I'd retrospectively apologize to the violet industry, but it was probably only lesbian customers that kept it going at all."

Many modern sapphics have reclaimed violets as a symbolic gift between lovers or a symbol of affiliation within the LGBT community. While the trend of gifting violets in the 1920s was borne partly out of a need to be covert, in modern times it remains a romantic gesture that honors the centuries of women-loving women who came before.

The Lavender Scare and the McCarthy Era

Joseph McCarthy was a United States senator from Wisconsin who had a tremendous amount of power in the 1940s and 1950s. A movement is even named after him, McCarthyism, otherwise known as the Second Red Scare. It was a strong political movement to oppress and persecute left-wing individuals and a campaign to spread fear of communist and Soviet influence on American institutions and of Soviet espionage in the United States.

World War II would not have been won if not for the uneasy alliance of the United States, Great Britain, and the Soviet Union. After the war, their political differences came rushing to the forefront. "Communism" became a curse word, with suspicions and outright paranoia infecting post-war America. Although its primary focus was on "outing" communist sympathizers, it was also directed at homosexuals or those who might possibly be homosexual.

"The Lavender Scare" refers to the identification and mass firings of thousands of homosexual people from the US federal government during the 1950s. This gay witch hunt grew out of the post-World War II Red Scare and its subsequent McCarthy-era campaign to purge communists from the government. McCarthy claimed that homosexuality was a psychological maladjustment leading people to Communism. The call to remove gay men and lesbian women from government employment was based on the theory that they were likely to be communist sympathizers and thus security risks.[1]

During Dwight Eisenhower's presidency (1953–1961), he did nothing to change or eliminate these laws. In his campaign against Adlai Stevenson, he refused to confront the unfounded lies about Stevenson being a gay man and they became weapons used against Stevenson. Walter Winchell, a rabid anti-Communist radio columnist, declared that "A Vote for Stevenson is a vote for Christine Jorgenson," referring to the first openly trans woman in the United States. In short, Christine Jorgensen was born George William Jorgensen Jr. in 1926. In 1944, Jorgensen was drafted into the US Army during World War II. After the war, she learned about sex reassignment surgery and traveled to Europe, where in Copenhagen, Denmark, she obtained special permission to undergo a series of operations beginning in 1952. Upon her return to the United States in the early 1950s, she became an instant celebrity, known for her directness and polished wit, and used the platform to advocate for transgender people. Her 1967 autobiography *Christine Jorgensen: A Personal Autobiography* sold almost 450,000 copies.[2]

The Lavender Menace

The phrase "lavender menace" was coined by National Organization for Women leader Betty Friedan, who used it at a NOW meeting in 1969, claiming that outspoken lesbians were a threat to the feminist movement an arguing that the presence of these women distracted from the goals of gaining economic and social equality for women. As explained earlier, the color lavender is associated with the LGBT/gay rights movement in general.[3]

Ironically, this exclusion of and challenge to those questioning heterosexuality was a major impetus for the creation of lesbian feminist groups and a lesbian feminist identity. Many feminists, not just Friedan, in NOW felt that lesbian issues were irrelevant to most women and would hinder the feminist cause and that identifying the movement with lesbians and their rights would make it harder to win feminist victories. Since many lesbians had found a comfortable activism at home within the rising feminist movement, this exclusion stung. It called into serious question the concept of "sisterhood." If "the personal is political," how could sexual identity, women identifying with women rather than with men, *not* be part of feminism?

By 1971, NOW included lesbian rights among its policies, and eventually lesbian rights became one of the six key issues NOW addressed. In 1977, at the National Women's Conference in Houston, Texas, Betty Friedan apologized for her promotion of excluding lesbians as "disrupters" of the women's movement and supported actively a resolution against sexual preference discrimination. When this passed, the Mississippi delegation hoisted signs saying, "Keep Them in the Closet." In 1991, newly elected NOW president Patricia Ireland stated her intention to live with a female partner. She remained president of the organization for ten years. NOW also sponsored a Lesbian Rights Summit in 1999.[4]

Revolutions for Deaf and LGBT Communities

Before the two defining moments of deaf and LGBT history—the Gallaudet "Deaf President Now!" revolution in March 1988 and the Stonewall riots in June 1969—the two communities held one thing in common: their marginalization.

Before the Americans with Disabilities Act of 1990, the Deaf community kept largely to itself. The watershed event for them would be, I believe, the Gallaudet Revolution in 1988, when deaf students boycotted until a president like them, deaf, was appointed. They had their own communities, their own support system, their own schools (albeit by that time largely residential *oralist* schools, which sought to deprive them of their natural sign and culture), and their own limited professions. Mainstream society mostly ignored them and to a large extent participated perhaps unconsciously in the Deaf community's de facto exclusion. The deaf had their own churches, their own community centers, and their jobs were, as noted before, out of the public view, such as in printing and other invisible-to-the-public work.

Gallaudet University, the world's only residential university for the deaf and hard-of-hearing, has a history of tension surrounding issues of language, identity, and the attendance of hearing students, including those with cochlear implants. The Deaf President Now (DPN) protest in 1988 highlighted the struggle for deaf leadership within deaf culture and identity. Some argue that cochlear implants are a form of oppression, while others see them as a tool for inclusion and access to the hearing world. We see this battle between the worlds played out in the deaf family of the Artinians, as shown in the video *The Sound and the Fury*. I believe it is an understandable first reaction to how in American history we shuttled deaf children off to deaf schools where they were not allowed to use sign language and most of their education, after the fateful Congress of Milan in 1880, chose to push oralism only.

In the homosexual community, there is another layer to its history that involves the very real threats of "coming out," such as incarceration; involuntary institutionalization in mental institutions; invasive medical treatments such as electroshock therapy, "conversion" therapy, and lobotomies; loss of child custody; and loss of jobs.

The term "homosexuality" is of recent origin. The word "homosexual" first appeared in German in an 1869 political pamphlet by Karl Maria Kertbeny[5] (the pseudonym of Karl Benkert) that intended to protest the inclusion of Prussian sodomy statutes (the legal antecedents of the infamous Nazi Paragraph 175) in the constitution of a unified German state. This, of course, does not mean that "homosexuality" is a recent occurrence. It goes back through recorded history, in virtually all cultures and times. Yet naming it as a reality, an ontology, that could adhere to a person and be an essential identifier of personhood—or lack of it—is fairly modern. Falsely based on nature's supposed dualism rather than simply describing a sexual behavior, the term identified a person as someone who could be separated, legislated against, criminalized, and ultimately demonized.

For the men, much of this commingling with other homosexuals, not yet an actual movement, occurred under the name of the Mattachine Society.[6] Commonly believed to have been named by Harry Hay (although there was an organization of the same name in Amsterdam by 1948),[7] who was inspired by a French medieval and masque group, it was originally a secret fraternity of unmarried townsmen who never performed in public unmasked and who went into the countryside to conduct dances and rituals, sometimes even turning into masked peasants protesting against oppression. The group was preceded by the Society for Human Rights, formed in 1924 in Chicago, whose purpose was to combat the public prejudices and "to promote and to protect the interests of people who by reasons of mental and physical abnormalities are abused and hindered in the legal pursuit of happiness which is guaranteed them by the Declaration of Independence, and to combat the public prejudices against them by dissemination of facts according to modern science among intellectuals of mature age."[8]

A complementary organization to the Mattachine Society, the Daughters of Bilitis, was formed by two women, Del Martin and Phyllis Lyon, in San Francisco in 1955. It became the first lesbian rights organization in the United States. The group was originally conceived as a social alternative to lesbian bars, which were considered illegal and subject to raids and police harassment. It lasted for fourteen years and became a tool of education for lesbians, gay men, researchers, and mental health professionals. The group's mission soon expanded to providing support to women who were afraid to come out. Its very establishment, with witch hunts and police harassment routinely occurring, was an act of courage; members always feared that they were under attack merely because of who they were. The name of the newfound club was chosen in its second meeting. "Bilitis" is the name given to a fictional lesbian contemporary of Sappho by French poet Pierre Louÿs in his 1894 work *The Song of Bilitis*.[9]

Although most lesbians and gays were still "in the closet" due to repercussions, including arrest, incarceration, and exclusion from jobs, the movement was building momentum and would soon break through the surface to explode into the public spotlight. Some brave few in the early 1960s engaged in picketing and sit-ins, identifying themselves in public. Focusing on building community, the San Franciscan Society for Individual Rights (SIR) was formed in 1964. In 1966, SIR opened the nation's first gay and lesbian community center.

Just a year before SIR was founded in 1966, there was a sit-in at Dewey's lunch counter in Philadelphia. Paralleling the successful sit-ins of the Civil Rights Movement, this one had an added twist: it involved transgendered African Americans protesting their exclusion by the management for wearing "non-conforming" clothing that the management claimed was driving away other customers. Of the 150 who showed up, four were arrested, charged, and ultimately convicted of disorderly conduct. The stage was slowly but surely being set for the Stonewall Revolution of 1969.

A Bird's-Eye View of Presidents and LGBT Protections: 1977 to 2024

There were a great many legislative acts in those years pertaining to the status of homosexuals. In the interest of brevity, I will highlight only the most important and impactful ones from each Presidential administration.

Jimmy Carter (1977–1981)
• The Civil Service Reform Act of 1978 offered an updated list of protected classes: by race, color, religion, sex, age, marital status, and handicaps. Noticeably, still absent was sexual orientation because of the possibility of blackmail and thus a security risk. The risk was still present for anyone perceived as gay who needed security clearance to work in top-secret jobs. In the McCarthy Era of the 1940s and 1950s after defeating the Axis powers in WWII, the focus was not only to weed out any people with either open or possibly secret ties to Russia but also homosexuals, because they would be open to threats and blackmail. In point of fact, many more perceived homosexuals lost their security clearances and jobs because they were known to be or believed to be gay.[10]

Ronald Reagan (1981–1989)
• In 1978, Reagan spoke strongly against the Briggs Initiative, which would have barred homosexuals from teaching in public schools. It had the potential of infringing on the basic rights of privacy and on constitutional rights.
• In 1982, the AIDS crisis reinforced anti-gay prejudice. AIDS treatment was negatively affected in an increasingly hardline approach. It was not until Reagan's second term, in 1987, that he gave his first major address on AIDS. To this day, his time in offices has mixed reviews. I still remember when I first met a gay man with AIDS at the Metropolitan Church in Portland, Oregon, in the 1980s. It was both a confusing and scary time. I did not know what to do with my feelings. It seemed as if he was on display.

The origins of AIDS can be traced to Central and West Africa. HIV, the virus that causes AIDS, is believed to have originated in chimpanzees in this region. It is thought that the virus crossed into humans from chimpanzees with infected blood or other bodily fluids. Peter Daszack with the EcoHealth Alliance claims that over 35,000,000 million people were killed by the virus.

It is intriguing to me to remember that the AIDS virus was originally not identified as a "gay disease." In fact, heterosexual activity is a major mode of HIV transmission in Africa, with a high percentage of infections in sub-Saharan Africa occurring through heterosexual contact. AIDS in Africa is primarily a heterosexual disease, with prevalence rates particularly high among younger women and women with multiple sexual partners.[11]

In general, the gay community sees Reagan's inaction in the face of a usually fatal disease inexcusable, especially since they as a whole group were unjustly blamed for the outbreak.

George H. W. Bush (1989–1983)

• In a refreshing note for the next Republican president, Bush signed the ADA in 1990, which protected people with HIV.

The summary below is taken from the "Guide to Disability Rights Laws."[12]

> The ADA (Americans with Disabilities Act) of 1990 protects individuals with HIV/AIDS from discrimination, as it considers these conditions to be disabilities that substantially limit one or more major life activities. This protection applies to individuals both with and without symptoms of the disease, and to those discriminated against because they are perceived as having HIV/AIDS. The ADA prohibits discrimination in employment, public accommodations, and state and local government services.
>
> Definition of Disability:
> The ADA defines a disability as a physical or mental impairment that substantially limits one or more major life activities. HIV and AIDS are considered such impairments, regardless of whether a person is symptomatic or not.
>
> Protection from Discrimination:
> The ADA prohibits discrimination against individuals with HIV/AIDS in various settings, including:
>
> Employment: Employers are prohibited from discriminating against qualified individuals with HIV/AIDS in hiring, promotion, or other employment decisions.

Public Accommodations: Businesses that are open to the public, like restaurants, stores, and movie theaters, are prohibited from discriminating against individuals with HIV/AIDS in providing services or access.

State and Local Government Services: State and local governments are prohibited from discriminating against individuals with HIV/AIDS in providing access to programs and services.

- Bush also supported the Ryan White CARE Act, the largest federally funded program for HIV and AIDS patients. Critics, however, claimed that each of these bills came about because of AIDS activist pressure rather than White House leadership. Critics still believe that Bush could have done much more for the AIDS crisis than his lukewarm reactions and responses.

Bill Clinton (1993–2001)
- In 1993, President Clinton issued Defense Directive 1304.26, "Don't Ask, Don't Tell," which directed that military applicants were not to be asked about their sexual orientation.
- In 1995, Executive Order 12968 stated that the US government was to end discrimination based on sexual orientation.

George W. Bush (1999–2007)
In his commentary on April 17, 2000, titled "Bush Miscalculates on Gay Republicans," Jonathan Rauch states that the President opposed their adoption rights and anti-discrimination protections and proposed a constitutional amendment forbidding same-sex marriage.[13] An article by Garance Franke-Ruta, published in 2013, "George W. Bush's Forgotten Gay-Rights History," says that Bush defied his party by endorsing civil unions in 2004. (But that same year, he backed a constitutional amendment forbidding same-sex marriage.)[14]

Barack Obama (2009–2017)
- The CIA was able to recruit openly gay employees.
- Obama extended limited benefits for same-sex domestic partners.
- The "Don't Ask, Don't Tell" policy, which prohibited openly gay men and women from serving in the military, was repealed by President Barack Obama after it was voted on and passed by both the House of Representatives and the Senate in December 2010. The repeal became effective on September 20, 2011.
- On June 26, 2015, the SCOTUS decision *Obergefell v. Hodges* allowed same-sex couples in the United States, no matter where they live, to have the same legal right to marry as different-sex couples.

On a personal note, after years of stops and starts, the *Obergefell* decision was thrilling for Sheryl and me. We were finally legally married in Berkeley, California, on November 2, 2008, several days before the anti-gay ballot passed that overturned legal marriage for gays. After seminary, we moved to Iowa rather than Nebraska because the Republican-controlled Iowa Supreme Court had ruled on April 3, 2009, that the Iowa Constitution forbids discrimination against same-sex couples. That ruling came just in time, since we moved there four months later. Iowa was the third state to do this, preceded by Massachusetts and Connecticut.

Sheryl and I were in Saint Louis at a Hearing Loop convention on June 26, 2015. When we took a break to go outside, the streets were full of Pride flags. We got to talk with several groups of young people who could have been our own grandchildren and were thankful that they would get to grow up in a safer world without sexual barriers.

Later that day, we walked down to see the famed arch. Across from it was the former courthouse where Roger Taney, the Chief Justice, issued his (in)famous ruling, the *Dred Scott* decision in 1857, that stated that people of Black African descent could not enjoy the rights and privileges conferred upon American citizens. The issue was that Dred Scott, an escaped slave, had managed to flee to Illinois, a free state. The ruling gave slave catchers the right to return him to Missouri, reasoning that he was still a slave.

The doors to the courtroom were open, and I got to sit in the seat where this decision came down. As I sat there and thought about the boundaries created against people for centuries, I gave thanks for my own life and the lives of others who were finally afforded the right to legally marry the ones they loved.

As I write this, I reflect on the motto, "Eternal vigilance is the cost of liberty." It is especially ironic now in light of the reversal of the 1973 *Roe v. Wade* decision by SCOTUS in *Dobbs v. Jackson Women's Health Organization* (2022). Women now have fewer rights than I did as a young person, and the attack on their personhood and rights to their own bodies continues to this day. This is personal for me. Sheryl and I have granddaughters whose essential freedoms have been taken away from them. The United States of America continues to regress in 2025, instigated perhaps by the presidency of Donald Trump, who is now in his second term.

Donald Trump (2017–2021)
• President Donald Trump's record with the LGBT community includes a long list of human rights violations. To help enact his agenda, he appointed anti-LGBT judges with alarming records to appointments at every level of the judicial system, including anti-equality Supreme Court Justices Gorsuch and Kavanaugh.

In the Workplace
• President Trump supported employment discrimination against LGBTQ people and banned transgender service members from the military—against the expert

advice of military leadership, medical authorities, budget analysts, 70 percent of Americans, and the armed forces of allied countries.

• Trump rolled back Obama-era non-discrimination protections. For example, the Department of Justice upended previous DOJ interpretations of the Civil Rights Act that protect transgender and nonbinary workers from employment discrimination.

• Trump's Department of Labor issued a regulation designed to allow federal contractors to claim a religious exemption to fire LGBTQ workers because of their sexual orientation or gender identity.

Health Care

• Trump advocated for the elimination of the entire Affordable Care Act. This move would jeopardize health care for more than 130 million people with preexisting conditions like HIV and eliminate non-discrimination protections for LGBTQ people.

• Trump created a Religious Discrimination Division whose sole purpose would be to defend physicians and other medical professionals who decide to refuse care, including to LGBTQ patients.

In Schools

• Trump suggested it is acceptable for schools to discriminate against LGBTQ students while accepting taxpayer funds.

• Then Secretary of Education Betsy DeVos rescinded Title IX rules related to schools' obligations to address sexual harassment, including sexual violence.

• Trump used Title IX to discriminate against transgender students when the Department of Education claimed that school policies allowing trans youth to participate in sports consistent with their gender identity violated federal law and threatened to withhold funds.

In Housing

• Trump allowed emergency shelters to deny access to transgender and gender-nonconforming people.

• Trump placed transgender incarcerated persons in the wrong prison.

In Families

• Trump allowed foster care programs to discriminate while accepting taxpayer funds and still receiving federal funding.

In Representation

• Trump's HHS proposed a new definition that would narrowly define gender as either male or female, unchangeable, and determined by birth.

• Trump eliminated information on LGBTQ rights, mentions, and representation on government websites.

In the World
• Trump refused LGBTQ asylum seekers fleeing violence.
• Trump urged US to leave the UN Human Rights Council over LGBTQ and other issues.

Joe Biden (2021–2025)
• President Biden repealed the ban on transgender military service.
• Pete Buttigieg was confirmed as Transportation Secretary, the first ever openly LGBTQ Cabinet member confirmed by the full Senate.
• The Fair Housing Act was enforced to protect LGBTQ people.
• The Department of Veterans Affairs expanded support for trans veterans, including a plan to end the ban on gender-affirming care for trans veterans.
• On March 31, 2021, the Department of Defense released detailed directives on reversing the transgender military ban set in place under Trump.
• The DOJ issued a memo on Title IX protecting LGBTQ students.
• The DOJ advocated for fair treatment of incarcerated transgender individuals.
• Biden enforced non-discrimination protections in health care.
• Biden called on Congress to pass the Equality Act.

While it is heartening to read in detail what the Biden administration did for LGBT rights, the battle is constant and changes depending on which party is in the White House. The different platforms of the two political parties, Democrats versus Republicans, often seem to support two opposite worldviews, the first of unity and the second of otherness. In 2024, Trump was elected president for a second term. Since then, he has attacked every group he can think of: LGBT, trans, seniors, and immigrants. He is trying to cut Medicare, Medicaid, and even Social Security. The fate of the nation rests in our hands. Which vision do we want for our country and for our world, the "Wholly Other" or the "Holy Other"?

The "devil" has many faces and is good at disguises. Defeating him requires all of us, in both our civic and personal lives, to continue to focus on love and unity rather than hatred and division.

Sitting Shiva: A Time to Mourn and a Time to Dance (Ecclesiastes 3:4)

(An Update)

I write this on November 7, 2024, two days after the presidential election. To say that the results stunned me, devastated me, and threw me and so many other beloved "holy others" into the pit of despair would be an understatement. There were no words for this loss, the impact of which will spread the messages of hatred and division throughout the world. My first thought was to go to bed with my comfort cats, pull the covers over my head, and lie there, hopefully forever.

But Sheryl and I chose to connect with friends like our clergy friend Kimberly, Fauna our Kenyan "daughter," and my son David, who wrote to me "I love you," while we openly shared our grief and confusion and feelings of being hopelessly lost. I and others felt profound loss, our compasses destroyed, everything ahead of us devastating, with no one to guide us to a now seemingly impossible and unattainable future.

Then I remembered a saying of one of the Berrigan brothers, Jesuit priests who were vocal opponents of the ill-conceived and ultimately lost Vietnam Conflict. "Don't just do something," they said. "Stand there!" Instead of rushing ahead in utter chaos or over a cliff like a herd of terrified lemmings, just stop! So I did. This brought back memories of my child Margaret's death from cancer in 1999 when she was only twenty years old. Financially, I had to go back to work immediately after losing her, but amid my work I was often swallowed by sorrow and grief. It was a blessing to have my own office with a lock on the door. I would turn the lock and crawl under the table, over which I had draped a blanket, curl up in a ball on the floor, and emerge only when I could find the courage to take the next step.

We Americans are not good at grief. When I was much younger, those who were grieving were permitted to wear a black armband in public to quietly acknowledge the grief process. Now we as a culture have given the official control of grieving to funeral directors, having them come to the home to take away the body, dress it for a public display of the deceased, and even supply a chaplain while the grieving family is tucked behind a screen so the rest of the mourners are not privy to their deep sadness and tears. Then there is a procession to the graveyard, already prepped by professional grave diggers, perhaps standing aside a bit impatiently while a clergyperson drones on and on with vacuous platitudes and the mourners stand silently, trying to hide their sobs. Even a newly minted widow might wear a black veil to shield herself from stares.

As I grappled with my emotions and thoughts, knowing that I was scheduled to preach a homily on Sunday only five days later, I was on the verge of telling my spouse that I had no words to say and could not do it. But as the day approached, I began to gather up my scattered and conflicting thoughts, and the title for my homily slowly but insistently emerged: "Sitting Shiva: A Time to Mourn and a Time to Dance." The theme comes from the book of Ecclesiastes, composed more than two millennia ago.

The practice of sitting shiva has survived for millennia within the Jewish community. After a body is prepared for burial, a place is set apart for those who are grieving. They enter one by one to sit together in silence or with softly spoken words for seven days. Some of the more orthodox among them may even rend their garments, signifying outwardly in their appearance that their lives are deeply affected by the loss, a gesture for all to see.

As if to affirm my still processing thoughts, the divine, be it accident or chance or a visible or invisible entity, showed up when we were watching one of our favorite shows that evening, *The Murdoch Murders*, with the action taking place in Toronto in the early part of the twentieth century. A Jewish man had just been murdered, and part of the action was to watch how his community sat shiva for him. Even as the body went in for an autopsy, a bearded rabbi sat in the room keeping shiva while the Western coroner opened the body of the deceased with her scalpel. Coincidence? Maybe, but I think not. It was a gentle nudge of encouragement from a loving universe that I was on the right path.

On the day when I assembled my thoughts, I took brief moments to play Words with Friends on my iPad. There too I found hidden messages. Ironically, but purposefully, as I played with several friends, jumping from one game to another, these next words by me emerged: "shiva," "dawn," "ping," "trek," "lien." I must admit that I have had my palm read, used a Ouija board, and done tarot cards, but mostly out of curiosity or interest so that I would take the results with a grain of sand.

But that day I took the time to examine the import and order of the seemingly randomly connected words I played with several players. Time to sit "shiva," as long as it takes. "Dawn" will come on its on schedule. I must admit that I was puzzled by the word "ping" but kept it in and searched out its meaning. It is a sharp sound, like the start of a race, a knock on the door. At some point in our journey, we will hear that ping and get to our feet, perhaps a bit unsteadily, to stumble into a new dawn, even while still rubbing our eyes, chasing the remnants of a dream, yawning to get out the last bit of sleep.

As we begin to awaken, we realize the next part of both our individual and community journeys to search for and welcome the "Holy Other" will not be, nor has it ever been, a simple walk in the park. It is a "trek," a South African word meaning a long, arduous journey, especially one made on foot, and, more often than not, into new, unexplored territory.

Like "ping," "lien" had me puzzled, but being essentially an honest person, I looked it up. I knew its literal meaning: a legal binding of one's personal property, holding it away from the person to access until a debt was cleared. It is easy to fall into the belief that we are now in bondage, slaves to an unjust and cruel slave owner, but we still own our own souls, our own hopes and dreams. Then, seemingly miraculously, came the word "qi," the vital energy or life force that lies within each person's inner core and that, as the word "lien" tells us, is still ours, untouched, undamaged, just waiting to be called up.

The last four words that revealed themselves were "wicks," "pew," "beg," and the double-edged sword, "bode." It made me think of the parable of the ten bridesmaids in Matthew 25, waiting for their master to come to them so that they can lead the procession to the bridal chambers, their lamps keeping the surrounding darkness at bay. Five of them are faithful, resting yet watchful, their wicks lit, waiting out the interminably long night. The other five fall into a slumber and awaken unprepared, their wicks burned out, and are left out of the wedding feast.

If we can stay awake together, encouraging one another, holding one another up when torpor seems to overcome us, the word "pew" arises. This is a bench traditionally known as a place of prayer, and we can find it not only at a religious service but also as a simple place to sit when we need a moment to recompose ourselves and perhaps search for a hope that seems to have vanished. We are called to sit in this proverbial pew together, holding up one another in our hearts. And then we "beg." There are traditionally four kinds of prayer: adoration, contrition, thanksgiving, and petition/intercession.

We revere or adore what is holy in each of us and all of us together, we examine our failings so that we can move on, we give thanks for our companionship and shared dreams, and then we "beg," or ask, for the healing of the world in its entirety, all the "wholly others" becoming "holy others," and we are all transformed in the process.

The last word that came up in my game was "bode." I immediately thought of two ideas: "bode" as something that can be good or bad, and "bode" as short for abode, the safe and welcoming place where we all come together and live. I intentionally pick the latter.

When our own time of shiva ends, may we turn to one another, huddle together, and get on with it! Let our mourning be over. It is time for us to dance. The world is waiting!

Notes

[1] For further information, see the book *The Lavender Scare: The Cold War Persecution of Gays and Lesbians in the Federal Government* by David K. Johnson (repr., University of Chicago Press, 2006).

[2] See "Christine Jorgenson," *Wikipedia*, https://en.wikipedia.org/wiki/Christine_Jorgensen.

[3] A well-known story about Abraham Lincoln when he was a young lawyer says that he shared not only a room but a bed with a fellow lawyer, Joshua Speed. Carl Sandburg (1878–1967), an American poet, biographer, journalist, and editor, commented on this relationship: "Lincoln and

Joshua Speed had streaks of lavender, spots soft as May Violets." See Sandburg, *Abraham Lincoln: The Prairie Years*, 1926.

[4] For a more detailed story of NOW's evolution, check out their website at https://now.org/resource/now-leading-the-fight/.

[5] Karl Maria Kertbeny, "Paragraph 143 of the Prussian Penal Code of 14 April 1851 and Its Reaffirmation as Paragraph 152 in the Proposed Penal Code for the Nordeutscher Bund. An Open and Professional Correspondence to His Excellency Dr. Leonhardt, Royal Prussian Minister of Justice" (1869).

[6] "Mattachine Society," *Brittanica*, http://www.britannica.com/EBchecked/topic/369619/Mattachine-Society.

[7] See Joan Roughgarden, *Evolution's Rainbow: Diversity, Gender, and Sexuality in Nature and People* (Berkeley: University of California Press, 2004).

[8] Jonathan Katz, *Gay American History: Lesbians and Gay Men in the U.S.A.* (New York: Crowell, 1976), 385–88, citing the Society for Human Rights, Inc., Chicago, charter signed December 10, 1924, certificate no. 8018, State of Illinois, Office of the Secretary of State, Commercial Department, Springfield, IL.

[9] For a complete history of the development of this movement, see "Daughters of Bilitis," *Wikipedia*, https://en.wikipedia.org/wiki/Daughters_of_Bilitis.

[10] For more, see "These People Are Frightened to Death," *Prologue Magazine* 48, no. 2 (Summer 2016), https://www.archives.gov/publications/prologue/2016/summer/lavender.html.

[11] For more, see Paul Sharp and Beatrice Hahn, "Origins of HIV and the AIDS Pandemic," *National Library of Medicine*, 2011, https://pmc.ncbi.nlm.nih.gov/articles/PMC3234451/.

[12] For the version updated February 28, 2020, see https://www.ada.gov/resources/disability-rights-guide/.

[13] See Rauch news clipping at https://archives.library.unt.edu/repositories/2/archival_objects/137517.

[14] See https://www.theatlantic.com/politics/archive/2013/07/george-w-bushs-forgotten-gay-rights-history/277567/.

Chapter 9
Psychological and Medical Treatments before the Revolutions

The real political task...is to criticize the working of institutions that appear to be both neutral and independent; to criticize them in such a manner that the political violence which has always exercised itself obscurely through them will be unmasked so that one can fight them. —Michel de Foucault, 1974[1]

When I became a graduate student in counseling at Oregon State University in 1992, the then-current Diagnostic and Statistical Manual, DSM-3, had upgraded the diagnosis of "homosexuality" from being a personality disorder to being a "psychosexual disorder." The first DSM, published in 1952 by the American Psychiatric Association, listed homosexuality as a "mental disorder." Following the 1969 Stonewall riots, gay activists challenged this diagnosis. In 1973, the board of trustees declassified homosexuality as a mental disorder, replacing it with ego-dystonic sexual orientation for gay people who were uncomfortable with being gay. The DSM-5, published in 2013 and still used today, includes no category that can be applied to people based on their sexual orientation.

Is it any wonder that my female classmates who were teachers had to lead double lives and live in daily fear of their "secret" being revealed and losing their jobs? As they became more comfortable being out, at least in class, one of them revealed that she had undergone conversion therapy in her earlier life. Evidently, it hadn't worked, because years later, I was invited to her wedding to another woman—a simple ceremony in their own backyard. "A small step for a woman. A giant step for humankind."

When I began my chaplain internship in 1986, I was taken on a tour of all the wards, including the one with sex offenders, which included both homosexuals and heterosexuals. We went to a room where I saw a recliner and a machine I did not recognize. It was a Penile Plethysmograph, whereby electrodes were attached to the penis to measure responses to different pictures. If there was arousal, the patient would get an electric jolt. It was called aversion therapy. I did research on the latest code of ethics for such a practice. With many modifications, including that the patient had to be over eighteen and give consent, it is still a legitimate form of practice, as well as the electric shock treatment.

As we can see in the following section, the psychological and medical establishment, masked "benevolently," claimed to be both neutral and independent. They were neither when it comes to these two populations—the Deaf and the homosexual.

Treatment of the Deaf

In the United States, the first Deaf school began in Hartford, Connecticut, in 1817, under the guidance of Thomas Gallaudet and Laurent Clerc. This was soon followed by the one in Philadelphia. In the articles of incorporation written in 1821, we can sense the full force of the way the hearing community viewed the plight of those born "deaf and dumb":

> Idiocy sometimes attendant, often consequent; —the natural powers of the mind exercised to their own perversion or destruction, the passions headstrong and impetuous, by the absence of control of judgement, — fretful impatience at the dark perception of unknown and unattainable excellence in the rest of their species, —the wily cunning of instinct in the place of generous wisdom, —total unfitness for all occupations but those to which the brutes are as well adapted, —an entire and invincible separation from the vast stores of knowledge which human talent has accumulated—ignorance of the truths of Revelation, her glorious assurances and unspeakable consolations, —all these are among the bitter ingredients that fill up the vast measure of affliction to the Deaf and Dumb.[2]

It is instructive to note the words "ignorance of the truths of Revelation" because this is connected to the underlying beliefs of the Gallaudets, both father and son, and Alexander Graham Bell. The elder Gallaudet, Thomas Hopkins, was a product of the Second Great Awakening, a Protestant religious revival from 1795 to 1835 that included camp meetings throughout the country. He was driven to communicate with the deaf and teach them language because he and his son truly believed that it was imperative for the salvation of the born-deaf to be able to "talk" with Jesus directly, without the need for a minister. W. A. Cochrane shows this religious ethnocentrism in these words:

> [W]e are called to labor among those who have no concept of a God; who know nothing of the kind, loving, merciful Father of the universe; whose ears have been closed to the simplest facts of Bible history; whose minds are shrouded in ignorance as dark as that which has settled down upon any of the nations of the earth.... The teacher's work is to lift the veil that shuts out the beauties and glories of heavenly Jerusalem...so that in time the pupil comes to understand the plan and need of redemption....[3]

As Harlan Lane shows, the medical and psychological establishment mimicked, in their own jargon, Cochrane's prejudices and distortions:

The sociologist Erving Goffman distinguishes three kinds of stigma: physical, characterological, and tribal.... All three categories of stigma are ascribed to deaf [and LGBT] people. Physically they are judged defective; this is commonly taken to give rise to undesirable character traits, such as concreteness of thought and impulsive behavior. Hearing people may also view deaf people as clannish—even, indeed, an undesirable world apart, social deviants like those Goffman lists.... In the hearing stereotype, deafness is the lack of something, not the presence of anything.... "Hearing people are called deaf, [add LGBT, "faggot," "queer,"] by extension, when they refuse to listen, especially to moral advice.[4]

Lane concludes with summarizing this approach, naming it *colonialism*:

Like the paternalism of the colonizers, hearing paternalism begins with defective perception, because it superimposes its image of the familiar world of hearing people on the unfamiliar world of deaf people. Hearing paternalism likewise sees its task as "civilizing" its charges: restoring deaf people to society. And hearing paternalism fails to understand the structure and values of deaf society. The hearing people who control the affairs of deaf children and adults commonly do not know deaf people and do not want to. Since they cannot see deaf people as they really are, they make up imaginary deaf people of their own, in accord with their own experiences and needs. Paternalism deals in such stereotypes. Like the colonizers and the colonized, the hearing establishment serving deaf people and deaf people themselves have two different points of view, two different conceptions of deaf people, and two radically different agendas in America.[5]

The Deaf and Eugenics

Alexander Graham Bell was a product of the secular enlightenment, whereby the needs of the individual must cede to those of the larger society in a kind of Social Darwinism that developed in the wake of Darwin's publication of the *Origin of the Species* in 1859. This policy of what would be called Social Darwinism was in place in the latter part of the nineteenth century.

When the federal government began in the 1880s to regulate immigration, the exclusion of what were termed "defectives" was one of the primary aims. Deaf people were among the thousands of disabled immigrants turned back each year at US ports as "undesirables." Stereotyped as economically dependent and carriers of potentially defective genes, deaf immigrants were seen as a threat to the nation. The advent of immigration restriction was one aspect of a pervasive and intensified stigmatization of disability during this period, which also saw the widespread incarceration of mentally disabled people in institutions, the sterilization of the "unfit" under state eugenic laws, the suppression of sign language, and a growing tendency to exclude disabled people from social and cultural life.[6]

Bell applied these theories to deafness, urging those born deaf not to intermarry, although he stopped short of advocating legislation to effect this. In the early twentieth century, this politically motivated Social Darwinism did result in laws that set up quotas for different immigrant groups, depending on their "desirability" and the nature of prejudice against them. Carol Padden and Tom Humphries encapsulate this involvement with eugenics:

> [In 1908] Charles Davenport praised Alexander Graham Bell's reputation as a scientist and asked if he would agree to serve on a committee on eugenics under the auspices of the American Breeders' Association, which had as its goal, among others, to determine the "precise law of mating ensuring normal offspring from a parent with hereditary tendency toward ear defect." Today deaf parents are referred to genetics counselors in order to determine whether they may have deaf children. Though deaf people are said to have the right to make their own decisions about whether to bear deaf children, there is always the threat of "social responsibility."[7]

During the Harding administration, eugenics was used specifically to slow the flood of immigrants to the United States—at least *some* immigrants.[8] The more thorough law signed later by President Coolidge established quotas based on national origins. College students, professors, and ministers were exempt, but people from some nations were prohibited from legal entry. Mexican laborers were initially allowed, but measures were quickly added to prohibit this because they were not eligible for citizenship. The measures were applied across the board to East Asians. The quotas were also set to favor a large number of newcomers from Britain, Ireland, and Northern Europe while restricting entry from Southern and Eastern Europe, all based on the faulty science of racial eugenics.

These hateful and faulty eugenics beliefs and policies were strongly influential in developing the Nazi party's eugenics policies in World War II. The Nazis had a policy of mandatory sterilization of many deaf people, sometimes without the benefit of anesthetics. This expanded to much more stringent policies when experimental gas chambers began to be tested on people in institutions, the mentally defective, deaf, and other social "undesirables."[9] In 1939, the Nazis began experimenting with poison gas for the purpose of mass murder with the killing of mental patients. A Nazi euphemism, "euthanasia" referred to the systematic killing of Germans whom the Nazis deemed "unworthy of life" because of mental illness or physical disability. "Euthanasia" is from the Greek, meaning "a good death." The question remains, for whom?

Jack Beckett describes one especially horrific Nazi method:

> One of several methods used was the gas van. Such vans were first deployed in 1940 in "Euthanasia" operations. Hitler delegated the "Euthanasia" operation to Reichsleiter Philip Bouhler, Dr. Karl Brandt, and several doctors of their choice. The targets were several German population groups: the mentally ill or retarded, the chronically ill, and criminals. At first, the murders were carried out in fixed, sealed chambers, into which carbon monoxide gas was pumped from metal canisters. In addition, some were killed by lethal injections and by shooting. Gas vans were first used in 1940, when Polish mentally ill children were locked in a sealed van and killed by carbon monoxide.[10]

While the oppression of deaf people in this country never descended to this level, it is important to remember that they were objects of colonialism, albeit, as Lane notes, masked "in benevolence." This has continuing implications on educational and medical issues that will be discussed later.

Treatment of Lesbians and Gays

Homosexuals, too, suffered from discrimination similar to that leveled against deaf people. It sometimes took the form of institutionalization, arrest, and conviction for sexual offenses (such as being homosexual), sterilization, and castration. Male homosexuals were targeted for the concentration camps in Germany, where a number of them ended up in the gas chambers. When the camps were liberated, they were kept in prison under the infamous Paragraph 175.

Paragraph 175 was a provision of the German Criminal Code from May 15, 1871, to March 10, 1994, that made homosexual acts between males a crime, and in early revisions the provision also criminalized bestiality. The statute was amended several times. The Nazis broadened the law in 1935; in the prosecutions that followed, thousands died in concentration camps. East Germany reverted to the old version of the law in 1950 and abolished it entirely in 1988. West Germany retained the Nazi-era statute until 1969, when it was limited to "qualified cases," and finally revoked it entirely in 1994 after German reunification.[11] While the number of homosexuals in concentration camps is hard to estimate, Richard Plant gives a rough estimate of the number of men convicted for homosexuality "between 1933 to 1944 at between 50,000 and 63,000."[12]

The US, the Eugenics Movement, and the Influence of Henry Ford

One would think that, seeing the atrocities in movie theatres and national headlines, this country would be loath to do anything even vaguely resembling the draconian measures inflicted on such a wide scale on so many different groups of "undesirables." Unfortunately, that is not so.

We can start before the beginning of World War I in Michigan. A number of immigrants flooded into the United States at the beginning of the twentieth century, and their number increased exponentially as the fallout of refugees from the war came to the US. At the same time, Henry Ford was expanding his plants rapidly as the Model T Ford, called the "Tin Lizzie," took hold of the nation's imagination. The days of horse-drawn carriages rapidly drew to a close and the Wright brothers in Kitty Hawk, North Carolina, began to make the fantastic imagining of writers like Jules Verne a reality.

Ford was not just a dreamer but an industrialist whose visions changed the course of the history of transportation. He also dreamed of a perfect society. In 1915, he persuaded his friend, Reverend Samuel Simpson Marquis, to leave his post as dean of St. Paul's Episcopal Cathedral in Detroit and come into the welcoming fold of Ford Motor Company with these words, "I want you, Mark, to put Jesus Christ in my factory!"

Ford was always cognizant of the conditions of the working man. He instituted an eight-hour day, a living wage, and often housing as well. This oversight also extended to the workers' up-to-then private home lives. To this end, Ford instituted a Sociological Department with a staff of more than fifty investigators, growing to a force of 160 men within two years. Their job was to establish standards of proper behavior throughout the company. To qualify for the higher wage, workers had to submit to exhaustive home inspections, show that they were sober (Ford was a teetotaler, non-smoker, and vegetarian), marry if cohabiting, have no roomers in their homes, save money on a regular basis, and have clean and orderly houses. If workers failed the home inspection, they were offered the opportunity for rehabilitation to become "lifted up" to the moral requirements for working at a Ford company. If they qualified, only then were they certified to receive Ford's "bonus-on-conduct."

As the post-war refugee boom continued, refugees flooded in from Poland, Croatia, Hungary, and Italy, including thousands of Jews. The Ford Motor Company, amid a great post-war expansion, needed these workers on the assembly lines in a number of newer plants. The new workers were required to attend compulsory Sociology Department classes. The goal was twofold: first, to teach them practical methods for speaking English; second, and equally important, to indoctrinate them with learning about the history and future of America, with a goal to make them US citizens as quickly as possible.

Ford was not alone in this vision. A consortium of major corporate players also worked towards these ends. The fervor of both evangelization and post-war patriotism led to the declaration of National Americanization Day being established on July 4, 1915, years before the end of World War I. On the surface, it sounds like a good idea to bind up the wounds of a world torn apart by wars, to integrate and support those whose livelihoods and homes were destroyed, but I personally believe that Ford took it to a dangerous and fanatical end. He decided to create a "Melting Pot" ceremony, first performed on July 4, 1915, to honor the First National American Day declared by corporations in Detroit in a special ceremony. It took place on a baseball field near Highland Park and included a brass band and Clinton DeWitt, the principal of Ford's school, dressed up as Uncle Sam. Ford's uniformity campaign was "to impress upon these men that they are, or should be, Americans, and that former racial, national, and linguistic differences are to be forgotten."[13]

With this ceremony, Ford made his disparate workforce as identical as possible to the Tin Lizzies when they were finished on the assembly line. As Neil Baldwin summarized,

> Henry Ford's Sociological Department and school flourished at a time when the ideal "national type" was fixed as if in amber. America's self-image in those tense days on the brink of World War I made full use of a "Transmuting pot" rather than a "melting pot," because all the ingredients of other national identities were compelled to become assimilated into an idealized "Anglo-Saxon model," more familiarly known as the American way of life. The messianic purpose of America in 1914, in Henry Ford's mind, was best expressed as a special kind of civic religion, and he was its chief minister.[14]

Ford was not only adamant about erasing the cultural and political history of his new workers but also outspokenly anti-Jewish, so he had no trouble working hand-in-glove with the Germans up to and during World War II to keep his automobile factories in Germany running full steam ahead during Hitler's reign of terror.

Protocols of the Elders of Zion and Henry Ford

Henry Ford distributed *The Protocols of the Elders of Zion*, a fictitious, antisemitic account of the goals of the "nefarious Jews," in his newspaper *The Dearborn Independent* (1919–1927). Lawsuits regarding antisemitic material published in the paper caused Ford to close it, and the last issue was published in December 1927.

This fraudulent document served as a pretext and rationale for antisemitism mainly in the early twentieth century. It purported to be a report of a series of twenty-four (twenty-seven in other versions) meetings held at Basel, Switzerland, in 1897 at the time of the first Zionist congress. This work of fiction was intentionally written to blame Jews for a variety of ills. Those who distributed it claimed that it was a document of a Jewish conspiracy to dominate the world. Jews and Freemasons were said to have made plans to disrupt Christian civilization and erect a world state under their joint rule. Liberalism and socialism were to be the means of subverting Christendom; if subversion failed, all the capitals of Europe were to be sabotaged. The conspiracy and its alleged leaders, the so-called Elders of Zion, never existed.

In his book written more than a century later in 2006, *The Plot: The Secret Story of the Protocols of the Elders of Zion*, Will Eisner examines the astonishing conspiracy and the fabrication of *The Protocols of the Elders of Zion*.[15] Presenting a pageant of historical figures from nineteenth-century Russia to today's ideologues, including Tsar Nicholas II, Henry Ford, and Adolf Hitler, Eisner unravels and dispels one of the most devastating hoaxes of the twentieth century.

I will admit that I have digressed a bit, but the treatment of the Jews was just another way of "othering." Like gays and deaf people, Jews were considered "undesirables." Hitler, even in his prison cell before emerging as the new chancellor of Germany in 1933, admired Henry Ford greatly, and his eugenics ideas were reinforced and solidified by Ford and his teachings. Hitler's Wolf's Den, where he and his mistress Eva Braun committed suicide in the closing days of World War II, contained some of the books Ford wrote and even had a portrait of Henry Ford hung in a place of honor on the wall. Both men had the goal or erasing those who seemed to have no value to the state, who stood out for their differences and were living reminders of an affront to the Übermensch or to the perfect American. Ford opened his plant in Cologne in 1940, collaborated in the war, and was awarded the Golden Grand Cross of the Order of the German Eagle with Swords, instituted on December 27, 1943, by Adolf Hitler. This diplomatic and honorary award was given to prominent foreigners, particularly diplomats, who were considered sympathetic to Nazism.

We need only look at the recent history of the American West Coast to see an only slightly milder version of eugenics being practiced. Laurence Cruz, in an article published in 2002, wrote, "[A]t least 2,648 people…were forcibly sterilized in Oregon between 1917 and 1981, most while in state care. Guided by the then-popular movement of eugenics, the idea was to prevent people with disabilities or criminal tendencies from passing on those and other traits deemed undesirable to their children."[16] He goes on to write that Oregon was one of thirty-three states that passed eugenics laws in the first quarter of the twentieth century. To accomplish this, the Oregon Legislature formed the State Board of Eugenics in 1923. This law permitted the sterilization of "persons, male or female, who are feeble-minded, insane, epileptic, habitual criminals, moral degenerates and sexual perverts, who are, or…who are likely to become, a menace to society."[17]

Chillingly, Oregon was not the worst offender—more than seven times as many people were sterilized in California—but the methods used in Oregon were more draconian than in many other states. In Oregon, castration was preferred over vasectomies, and the law initially was used to punish homosexuals. Until reforms in 1967, sterilization was often used as a condition of release from state institutions. The legislature did not abolish the Board of Eugenics until 1983.

As I researched, I remembered the story of a friend who was caught up in this medical model of labeling lesbianism as a sexual deviation that could be treated. This is Sally's response to my request for more information: "Some of my friends try to fit me into that mold of lesbians automatically being electro-shocked because of who they were.… I never did get that sense at all. What I observed was everyone on the ward routinely getting this form of treatment, regardless of their individual situation."

Sally revealed that she was in college when she began going to a psychiatrist in 1955 to be converted into a heterosexual. She was also having manic episodes, mixed with pills that were "zonking" her out, in her words. Her grades began to plummet, and she started to crash. She tried to self-medicate as well, using thyroid tablets, Dexedrine, coffee. In addition, she wanted to pursue a career as a public schoolteacher, where open homosexuality would preclude hiring and certainly expedite at-will firing. At the advice of her psychiatrist, Sally self-referred to the state mental hospital in Salem, Oregon (where I did two units of Clinical Pastoral education in the early 1980s and had a chance to witness an electroshock treatment of a patient on one of my wards, a young woman in her twenties who was schizophrenic and severely depressed).

During the several months of Sally's stay, she endured electroshock treatments:

> As nearly as I can remember some fifty years later, I had a course of about 10 "zaps" of shock treatment, and in those days, there were no preceding injections of anything to induce unconsciousness before the jolt. The shock procedure included getting up on the padded gurney, having several hard pillows placed under the small of my back, something hard and rubbery being placed between my teeth, several attendants applying Vaseline to my temples, then holding me just before Dr. Thompson lightly pressed

two terminals to my temples, and I would lose consciousness. Prior to our turn, we waited in a little room with dark green Naugahyde-upholstered couches, where we could see earlier unconscious patients being wheeled out from the "Shock Room," as we called it. We didn't see any convulsive movements, as patients weren't wheeled out until the convulsing had stopped. In fact, I didn't know until I read up on shock treatment much later there were any convulsions.[18]

Sally was there for three and a half months, coming in on a "high" and leaving in a deep depression. She was discharged on both Thorazine and Miltown simultaneously. Gradually, as an outpatient under the care of another psychiatrist, she was weaned from the medication and returned to school. She then switched to business school and began the process of "coming out."

It is impossible to sort out all the strands of Sally's life—depression, mania, self-medication, sexual identification. Yet one must wonder how much of her diagnosis and treatment, including shock therapy, stemmed from the complicity between the medical establishment and society in both judging and going to great lengths to "fix" her incipient lesbianism. During my two-year CPE experience I had befriended a psychiatrist, another lesbian. She had to be especially careful of hiding her sexual orientation when she worked with a patient on the violent offender ward.

Getting back to the "bigger picture" in Oregon, Cruz shows the board's wide "discretion" in using sterilization as a threat and a "solution" for many groups:

> The debate over an apology has uncovered decades of lost records and unknown cases, including at least 100 teenage girls forcibly sterilized—some simply for misbehaving — while they lived at the state training school for delinquent girls before 1941. Evidence of other cases has been obscured by the confidentiality of medical records and by the fact that the records of the Board of Eugenics and its successor, the Board of Social Protection, were lost or destroyed. At least one woman died as a result of a forced hysterectomy. The last-known state-ordered sterilization was in 1978.[19]

As I bring this section to a close, I want to point out that these treatments—electroshock therapy, conversion therapy, even lobotomies—were common practice, not just in the United States but in Europe as well. This is important to note in our own history as a country because of the role a British citizen, Alan Turing, a mathematician, logician, and computer scientist, played in ending World War II. The Germans had developed what they called the Enigma code to send secret, highly sensitive messages to the German military. Turing broke their code in 1942. The Germans never found out, which gave the allies a great edge, helping them to finally win the war several years earlier than it was predicted to end, saving millions of lives.

After the war, it was a different story. One would have imagined large ticker-tape parades in Turing's honor, especially since he was also the founder of Artificial Intelligence. But in 1952, Turing's home was burglarized, and upon investigating the robbery, the police found evidence of his homosexual relationship with another man. Turing was convicted of this "crime" and given the choice of a year in prison or chemical castration. He chose the latter. The castration drug was the use of chemicals or drugs to stop sex hormone production. After the treatment, Turing suffered several side effects, such as abnormal growth of mammary tissue. Turing's reputation continued to suffer after his arrest, and he was permanently disqualified from government code-breaking work. A year later, Turing committed suicide by taking a lethal dose of cyanide. He was only forty-two years old.

It took nearly sixty years for Turing to receive the respect in death that he never received in life. In 2009, British Prime Minister Gordon Brown offered an apology for the government's treatment of Turing, prompted by an online petition signed by 30,000 British citizens to clear Turing's name. A movie was made of his life story, *The Imitation Game* (2014). This is a complicated subject that deserves much more detailed observations and reflections. Yet I have shown the lengths to which both psychologists and medical doctors would go to "treat" what they considered pathologies. Simply being gay or rumored to be gay was enough to launch a swift and uncontested ousting from government work because it was thought that such people were more susceptible to pressures from enemies who wanted to garner state secrets from them.

Notes

[1] In Harlan Lane, *The Mask of Benevolence: Disabling the Deaf Community* (San Diego, CA: DawnSign Press, 1999), epigraph.

[2] *An Account of the Origin and Progress of the Pennsylvania Institution of the Deaf and Dumb* (Philadelphia: Harvard, 1821).

[3] W. A. Cochrane, 1873, quoted in James Woodward, *How You Gonna Get to Heaven if You Can't Talk with Jesus: On Depathologizing Deafness* (Silver Spring, MD: T. J. Publishers, Inc.,1982), 13, 14.

[4] Lane, *Mask of Benevolence*, 6-8.

[5] Ibid., 44.

[6] Douglas C. Baynton, "'The Undesirability of Admitting Deaf Mutes': U.S. Immigration Policy and Deaf Immigrants, 1882–1924," *Sign Language Studies* 6, no. 4 (Summer 2006): 391-415.

[7] Carol Padden and Tom Humphries, *Inside Deaf Culture* (Cambridge, MA: Harvard University Press, 2005), 176.

[8] See "Immigration Act of 1924," http://www.u-s-history.com/pages/h1398.html.

[9] See Donna F. Ryan and John S. Schuchman, eds., *Deaf People in Hitler's Europe* (Washington DC: Gallaudet University Press, 2002).

[10] Jack Beckett, "The Horrific Nazi Gas Vans—The Mobile Gas Chambers," *War History Online*, Aug 28, 2015, https://www.warhistoryonline.com/world-war-ii/the-horrific-nazi-gas-vans-the-mobile-gas-chambers.html.

[11] See "Paragraph 175 and the Nazi Campaign against Homosexuality," *US Holocaust Memorial Museum* (Encyclopedia), https://encyclopedia.ushmm.org/content/en/article/paragraph-175-and-the-nazi-campaign-against-homosexuality.

[12] Richard Plant, *The Pink Triangle: The Nazi War Against Homosexuals* (Washington, DC: New Republic Books, 1986).

[13] Neil Baldwin, *Henry Ford and the Jews: The Mass Production of Hate* (Public Affairs, 2001).

[14] Ibid., 42.

[15] Will Eisner, *The Plot: The Secret Story of the Protocols of the Elders of Zion* (W. W. Norton & Co, 2006).

[16] Laurence Cruz, "Eugenics Yields Dark Past," *Statesman Journal*, December 1, 2002.

[17] Ibid.

[18] Personal email correspondence with Sally, March 18, 2009.

[19] Cruz, "Eugenics Yields Dark Past."

Chapter 10
Horizontal Oppression and "Passing"

The idea of "passing" as a certain way when you are actually another is a tricky issue for me. When I lost my hearing overnight, I did not have a chance to "fake" it. I was suddenly and abruptly tossed out of the hearing world, and even now I can only return on my day-by-day hearing "visa," revocable at any moment. This, therefore, was not something I could hide, even if I wanted to. I was deaf. I am still deaf. Barring a miracle, I will die deaf.

The way it has come up for me personally is mostly in my work with both hearing people and hard-of-hearing people. Sheryl and I own the business together, meet regularly, and, when I do accompany her, I get to serve as the deaf person to see how the hearing loop is working. Sometimes I also do presentations, using my "deaf" poems, to give a human face to being deaf, not just to explain the technology. First, it is difficult to convince people with so-called "normal" hearing about the numbers of people with hearing loss and that there is a way to make their venue more accessible if they choose. Second, most people with hearing loss try to conceal it as long as they can, believing it cannot be changed.

I was not afforded that luxury. I lost all my hearing suddenly and totally unexpectedly. My "deaf" poems often voice my sadness, despair, and hopeless. Once I came to grips with this, which took close to a year, I embraced my new identity as a deaf woman with a sound processor and realized that I would have to continually fight like hell to be included in the hearing community. Rarely a day goes by that I do not have to advocate for myself. For instance, in September 2024, Sheryl and I decided to go to the presidential debate with a group of other Democrats. I asked ahead if it would be captioned, and the organizer of the event said that she would see to it. But when we got there early, as we always do to check out access, we learned that she had forgotten, so I had to ask the bartender to do it and then arrange my seat so I could see the captioning at the bottom of the screen.

My "coming out" was a more gradual process than my hearing loss. I did not even realize it myself at first, when I went to counseling for another concern. It took half a year of counseling, with the counselor continuing to probe me with questions about my sexuality. I think she realized I might be a lesbian well before I did. I knew this about some friends before they even began to question their own sexuality. My closest friend, married to another woman for a quarter of a century, was engaged to be married to a man when I first met her.

When I finally got there, I came out to my family, and we all went into family therapy. After I left the Catholic church because I knew I would never be allowed to use all the gifts of ministry that God had given me, I applied and was accepted to Pacific Lutheran Theological Seminary in Berkeley. And then I realized I had a second strike against me. As I was discovering that I was a lesbian, the Lutheran Church had not even begun to address the issue of LGBT inclusion. Even now, the Lutheran pastor in a nearby town, despite the denomination's full acceptance of LGBT people (even to ordination), was told by his board that he would not be allowed to perform same-sex weddings.

The only time I faced hearing and LGBT discrimination at the same time was at AlAnon, which I attended because a close family member was in AA. I went full throttle, as is my style, and got a sponsor…until she told me I should not tell anyone that I was married to another woman. Then she insisted I go to AA and Al-Anon meetings that had no hearing access for me and expected me to sit there and smile and nod my head. Thus, she expected me to go to meetings where I couldn't hear and also not tell anyone I was married to another woman! She was talking to the wrong person! I knew dysfunction when I saw it and fired her. We now have a big Pride flag attached to our front porch for anyone to see.

Is it any wonder, after reading about heterosexist and audist[1] prejudices and discrimination, that someone in either the LGBT or the Deaf community might be tempted to try to "pass" or engage in horizontal oppression? The LGBT person may try to pass both because of the real and still legal discrimination faced in the workplace, in families, in communities of faith, and in general society (especially with the current presidential administration). Those who discriminate view this person's life as a perversion, a sin, a moral failure, a contagion, a danger to society. This often results in a totally separate public life and private life—the person basically lives two lives.

When these artificial barriers collapse, it is then tempting to engage in horizontal oppression to try to "fit in" with the larger society. There is an attempt to accept the greater society's norms without critical evaluation: "We believe in the family, monogamy, the white picket fence, the American dream—the only difference is that we do not want you to do it with a partner of the same gender." A social hierarchy is set up to avoid difficult questions and present sexual identity and orientation as a "minor" detail, a footnote. President Clinton's directive to the military is a good example. The "Don't Ask, Don't Tell" policy allowed people to serve in the military without revealing that they were gay. How would heterosexuals feel about not being allowed to show pictures of their girlfriends or boyfriends, pictures of their families, letters from home?

Within the Deaf community, discrimination is more nuanced. Of course, there are gradations of deafness, including the hard-of-hearing and late-deafened who grew up in the hearing world, who have speech, and whose first language is not ASL. Gradual loss of hearing is often minimized or even denied. As for the truly deaf, you may well ask, how can a deaf person "pass" as hearing? What would they gain by horizontal oppression? And yet it can be done if one is determined enough. A case in point is the wife of Alexander Graham Bell, the inventor who threw himself into the oralist camp while eschewing sign language. Bell, who as a young man worked with deaf students, ended up marrying one. His wife Mabel was born hearing but lost this faculty around the age of five due to a childhood illness. Yet the stigma of deafness was such that she covered it up as well as she could:

> Passing can be exhausting: each situation requires its own brand of cunning and contains its own threats of disclosure. Some people must be avoided, especially similarly stigmatized people, while accomplices must be recruited. "I shrink from any reference to my disability," Mabel Bell wrote near the end of her life, "and won't be seen in public with another deaf person.... I have striven in every way to have [my deafness] forgotten and to be so completely normal that I would pass as one. To have anything to do with other deaf people instantly brought this hard-concealed fact into evidence. So, I have helped other things and people...anything, everything but the deaf. I would have no friends among them."[2]

The only deaf person Mabel related to was her mother-in-law, Eliza, who, like her, had been born hearing but also lost most of her hearing in early childhood. Eliza, too, refused to be seen in public with other deaf people and relied on an ear trumpet and the speech she had retained after her deafness to communicate with others. Lane concludes, "The more the deaf person internalizes the identity of *'hearing-impaired'* proffered by the audist establishment, the more he lends himself to its designs."[3]

This plays out in horizontal oppression by which deaf people have felt and been treated as inferior for generations. With the toehold gained by the Conference of Milan in 1880 and the persistent and unrelenting pressure Bell put into the oralist-only method, oralist schools and oralist values pushed out and almost exterminated sign language, deaf history, and deaf culture. There has been a rebound in these areas, including a surge of interest in sign largely due to the work of William Stokoe, whose linguistic analysis of ASL allowed it to take its rightful place with other languages as a proper, respectable, fully formed language rather than a "bastardized" version of English. Still, both society at large and the medical establishment in particular have put tremendous pressure on people with deaf children to "fix" them, especially by lowering the age of cochlear implants for children (now less than two years old) or shoehorning them into mainstreamed classes without proper support and without understanding the often-dire consequences for now effectively isolated deaf children.

The societal place that both the LGBT and deaf communities have sought and richly deserve is still shadowed by heterosexist and audist establishments that continue to cast their shadows over both groups.

Notes

[1] "Audism" is the belief that people with hearing are superior to those who are either deaf or hard-of-hearing. This includes both prejudice and outright discrimination.

[2] Harlan Lane, *The Mask of Benevolence: Disabling the Deaf Community* (San Diego, CA: DawnSign Press, 1999), 98.

[3] Ibid.

Chapter 11
Stonewall and After: The Match that Ignited a Revolution, June 27, 1969

It seems human nature to grow complacent and inattentive when an issue seems resolved once and for all. A glaring example is the overturning of *Roe v. Wade*, established in 1973, by the 2022 *Dobbs* decision. Now females have even less control of their bodies than they did in the seventies…and thus the fight goes on! It easily became one of the third rails of the politics of the 2024 presidential election. Does a fertilized sperm have more rights than a female between the age of menstruation, as low as ten, until menopause decades later? Sadly, for now it seems to be up to each individual state, making women's rights, safety, and even our lives appear like a checkerboard of which states do and do not treat us as sentient beings in charge of our own bodies and lives.

This reminds me of something that happened a few years ago in a small town in southwestern Iowa. There was a "Christian" group located in Omaha, just twenty miles away from our town across the Missouri River. Their latest target was Muslims. Sheryl and I decided we needed to protest against a supposedly Christian group being virulently anti-Muslim. Ironically, the meeting was in a community center right across the street from a Christian Church (Disciples of Christ) church, our own denomination, in the small town of Oakland, Iowa. We dressed in stoles signifying we were clergywomen standing up to hate. Some of the protesters went inside with newspapers, sat down with the crowd, and never looked up at all but kept reading newspapers as the speakers droned on. We were outside with the other protesters. I had originally thought the woman standing to my right wearing a headscarf was a cancer survivor, but as we began talking, she told me she was Jewish. She was standing in solidarity with us against islamophobia.

As the event ended, both protestors and participants came streaming out, for a few moments forced to mingle. We had ice cream for anyone who had attended, including the participants, but they all refused our good-willed gestures. When an older man was asked why he was there, he told us while hurriedly trying to get to his car that he was afraid that Muslims would break into his home and murder him and his wife.

As I saw the diverse mix of the people who had come to protest, I felt encouraged. To my knowledge, no Muslims were there but simply people from all walks of life concerned for the welfare and lives of their neighbor.

It had taken me a while to understand that we need to stand together, or we will fall apart. One of my early protests after my receiving my master's in counseling degree from Oregon State University was the "Walk for Love and Justice" I attended in June 1992 against homophobic ballot measures in the state of Oregon. In trying to confront the whole world, we witnessed the kindness and generous acts of those not identifying as gay break down our highly defended ramparts, and we emerged stronger and more united.

By the time Sheryl and I were at the pro-inclusion sit-in on the street of San Francisco in 2008, we—clergy, seminarians, and some others—were all already united. It did not matter what our sexual orientation was. That no longer made a difference. This sit-in was in response to Proposition 8.

Proposition 8, known informally as Prop 8, was a California ballot proposition and a state constitutional amendment intended to ban same-sex marriage; it passed in the November 2008 California state elections and was later overturned in court. The proposition was created by opponents of same-sex marriage in advance of the California Supreme Court's May 2008 appeal ruling, *In re Marriage Cases*, which followed the short-lived 2004 same-sex weddings controversy and found the previous ban on same-sex marriage (Proposition 22, 2000) unconstitutional. Proposition 8 was ultimately ruled unconstitutional by a federal court (on different grounds) in 2010, although the court decision did not go into effect until June 26, 2013, following the conclusion of proponents' appeals.

Sheryl and I decided to get legally married in the six-month hiatus in California allowing same-sex marriage. Although it was overturned days after the march, it did not invalidate the marriages of the 18,000 lesbian or gay couples who legally married during that small window of opportunity.

This famous quotation summarizes all these protests and marches for unity:

First they came for the socialists, and I did not speak out—
Because I was not a socialist.
Then they came for the trade unionists, and I did not speak out—
Because I was not a trade unionist.
Then they came for the Jews, and I did not speak out—
Because I was not a Jew.
Then they came for me—and there was no one left to speak for me.

This quote is attributed to Martin Niemöeller (1892–1974), a prominent Lutheran pastor in Germany. In the 1920s and early 1930s, he sympathized with many Nazi ideas and supported radically right-wing political movements. But after Adolf Hitler came to power in 1933, Niemöeller became an outspoken critic of Hitler's interference in the Protestant Church. He spent the last eight years of Nazi rule, from 1937 to 1945, in Nazi prisons and concentration camps. His famous quote is etched on his tombstone.

My personal hope is that anyone reading this book understands that it is not simply about the exclusion of LBGT and deaf people but about any group that is without thought or conscience preemptively excluded. Niemöeller was not Jewish, but he was able to see the Jews' true humanity and Holy Otherness. Niemöeller paid with eight years in a Nazi prison camp. What are we willing to endure for Holy Others?

Trying to capture LGBT history after the Stonewall riots is like taking a photo of someone jumping off a diving board. There is a moment when the "action" is captured, but the momentum carries it forward so fast that, by the time the film is developed, the momentum has taken it exponentially to its next flash point. As shown in the previous section, the ground was being laid for a "defining moment" in the Gay Revolution. More and more individual and group actions happened across the nation to "prime the pump," but the actions of a few patrons at a gay bar on June 27, 1969, were the gay equivalent of the "shot heard round the world" in Emerson's 1837 poem *Concord Hymn*, which immortalized in poetry the battle at Old North Bridge in Concord, Massachusetts, on April 19, 1775, between the colonists and the British army.

The "sound" was not that of a rifle shot behind a hedgerow abutting a country lane but of coins thrown by ejected patrons in mockery of the notorious system of payoffs that lined police officers' pockets as they sometimes turned a blind eye to these places of supposed affront to public morals. The violence escalated as the police tried to lead some of the customers into the all-too-familiar paddy wagons. Someone tried to ignite the inn after the surrounded police officers had taken shelter in the now-vacated bar. Others tossed bottles and bricks or set fire to trash cans.

As word spread throughout Greenwich Village, hundreds of gay men and lesbians—Black, white, Hispanic, mostly working class—joined the fray, invoking the summoning of the Tactical Patrol Force, a crack riot-control squad specifically trained to disperse crowds protesting the Vietnam War. Yet, unlike previous smaller confrontations, the crowd refused to disperse, simply ebbing and flowing to avoid the billy clubs of the increasingly frustrated and angry police force. The crowning insult came when a group of mocking drag queens formed a Rockettes-style chorus line to sing at the top of their sardonic voices:

We are Stonewall girls
We wear our hair in curls
We wear no underwear
We show our pubic hair…
We wear our dungarees
Above our nelly knees![1]

For five days the rioting continued, but by the time the final trash can fire was extinguished and the last shards of glass swept from the streets, the "closet" door had been literally wrenched from its moorings. Although it was theoretically possible to hide in the corner, it would never be as dark as before. "Come out, come out, wherever you are" was becoming a reality that more and more of the LGBT community would take as their own.

A number of possibly equally important events and issues have propelled the LGBT community to further activism and progress in the decades since Stonewall. One cannot speak about gay history without mentioning the contributions of Harvey Milk, a gay businessman who won a seat as a city supervisor in San Francisco in 1977. Milk served eleven months in office and was responsible for passing a stringent gay rights ordinance for the city. On November 27, 1978, Milk and Mayor George Moscone were assassinated by Dan White, another city supervisor who had recently resigned but wanted his job back. This happened just weeks after Milk successfully spearheaded an effort to defeat Proposition 6, also called the Briggs Initiative, named for a conservative state legislator from Orange County. This initiative would have banned gays and lesbians, and possibly anyone who supported gay rights, from working in California's public schools. It one of the efforts in a conservative movement that began with a campaign headed by former Mouseketeer Anita Bryant and her organization Save Our Children in Dade County, Florida, to repeal a local gay rights ordinance.

Shortly after this victory, AIDS was first diagnosed in 1981 in five homosexual men from Los Angeles. Initially seen as the "gay men's disease," it decimated the gay community. For years it was considered specifically and exclusively a gay epidemic, but now trends—and most attitudes—have shifted. It has crossed all sexual, cultural, class, and national barriers. While it is, of course, still a concern within the gay community, it no longer has the same sting, the same stigma, it had in the 1980s.

Three of the most hotly contested issues in the 2020s are continuing to add sexual orientation to hate crimes legislation; adding sexual orientation to national laws banning discrimination in jobs, housing, reproduction, and parenting; and upholding LGBT domestic partnership and marriage rights. This last one will be discussed later because it brings up the important debate over the purpose and nature of marriage. With the 2024 presidential election results, it is easy to imagine the rolling back and eliminations of rights for LGBT people, including marriage, adoption, job security, medical coverage for same-sex couples…and the list goes on and on.

Conclusion
"Eternal vigilance is the price of liberty"

As I edited this chapter, I heard rumors that even the Stonewall National Monument in New York City and other references to transgender and queer people were removed on the National Park Service website. Gay and trans patrons risked their bodies and lives to protest the billy club-wielding police raiding their private club. That was the whole point of the national monument: to honor their sacrifice. One article says,

> Protesters gathered at the Stonewall National Monument in New York City…after references to transgender and queer people were removed on the National Park Service website. The backlash came after President Donald Trump signed an executive order proclaiming the federal government only recognizes two sexes. While the trans flag still flies outside the Stonewall in Greenwich village, where the LGBTQ+ rights movement was born decades ago, the federal website dedicated to it has shortened the acronym to 'LGB,' for lesbian, gay, bisexual. Protesters rallied outside the Stonewall Inn declaring trans and queer people would not be pushed back into the shadows. 'We cannot be erased by removing words from a website,' said Samy Nemir Olivares, a protester who identifies as nonbinary. 'It's saying that trans and nonbinary and queer people do not exist at all.'"[2]

My hope for this book is not that it becomes a footnote in another book, covered with dust in a back corner of a library. I intend it to be a clarion call for all of us who have consciences, who still believe in the not-yet-realized dream of the best of us. This is no time to be silent. No time to be uncommitted. Future generations are waiting for our response.

Notes

[1] Lionel Wright, "The Stonewall Riots—1969," *Socialist Alternative*, July 1, 1999, https://www.socialistalternative.org/1999/07/01/the-stonewall-riots-1969-a-turning-point-in-the-struggle-for-gay-and-lesbian-liberation/.

[2] Ali Bauman and Kristie Keleshian, "Protests at Stonewall National Monument after 'LGBTQ' Changed to 'LGB' on Government Website," *CBS News*, February 15, 2025, https://www.cbsnews.com/newyork/news/stonewall-national-monument-protest-trans-queer-references-removed/.

Chapter 12
The Deaf Revolution: Gallaudet and "Deaf President Now!" March 6, 1988

My 2022 book, *Between the Deaf and Hearing Worlds: Blazing My Own Trail*, is based on the journal I kept, the poems I wrote, extensive notes from the medical staff (since I could not hear them), and our own lives on the seminary campus, which evidently had never had a deaf student. We had to advocate and educate for the ADA-required service of a real-time captioner who sat beside me in class at first. Then we had to educate the IT team to teach them about hearing loops and learn together how to install them. I chose this picture for my book cover because, unlike a path into a forest, where there would be ready food for those with trained eyes, I was metaphorically going into a heartless desert, with neither water nor food nor shelter.

At the time, I must have heard news about the Gallaudet student protests, but I did not remember them impacting me at all. I did not know any deaf person, but I know myself well enough to recognize that I would have supported their claiming of their own power. I had already been "out" as a lesbian for three years before the Stonewall Riots, so I was involved in learning about and supporting gay rights. When it comes to deaf issues, however, I believe that, like most people, I had not even thought of them. I lived in what Catholic moral theology would have called "ignorance." Once I did learn about something, if I continued to ignore it, it would then be called "invincible ignorance."

I do remember a time when I tried to bridge the gap. I was taking a class on homiletics at the American Baptist Seminary of the West in Berkeley, California. This was a sister school of Pacific School of Religion. It was filled with only hearing students, except for me. They had all become accustomed to passing the microphone from hand to hand before they spoke, because it sent the sound directly and wirelessly to the temporary hearing loop the IT team had to set up and take down for each class I attended. I decided to make part of my homily for the class a cross-cultural trip. I took the well-known Psalm 139, and instead of saying it out loud, I had the lights turned down for dramatic effect and then signed the psalm, with Sheryl standing by the edge of the class reading it. The first line is what I signed, and the second is what Sheryl read:

> If I ask darkness cover me
> If I asked darkness to cover me, also
> And light become night around me,
> And light to become night around me,

That darkness would not be dark to you,
That darkness would not be dark to you,
Night would be as light as [same as] day
Night would be as light as day
Not talk not speech
No utterance at all, no speech,
No sound people can hear
No sound that anyone can hear
Still night/day voice goes over all earth
Yet their voice goes out through all the earth
Night/day message goes end world
And their message to the ends of the world.

The homily was well received, but I knew that the lesson had not been apparent to me until I myself was struck deaf. Even in this age of information, it is possible to know about a major issue, such as global warming. Yet once we learn about it and still choose to do nothing about it, we are swimming in dangerous waters. It is a lesson for all of us to pay attention to the world, to be proactive, to be educated, and then to act. One of my favorite quotes, from a now-forgotten person, is "Preach the gospel always. Then, if necessary, use words." No more "thoughts and prayers"! They are not even worth the breath it takes to say them.

As mentioned earlier, the watershed event for the deaf that paralleled that of Stonewall for the LGBT revolution was the "Deaf President Now!" protest that began on March 6, 1988. An important development, however, primed the pump for the floodwaters of deaf liberation to sweep not only the campus of Gallaudet in the nation's capital but the whole country. It occurred a couple of decades before this revolt and involved the groundbreaking work of William Stokoe in methodically and persistently investigating the linguistic structures of ASL.

William Stokoe's role cannot be overestimated. Until he became a teacher of Chaucer at Gallaudet in 1955, American Sign Language was considered by all, both hearing and deaf, as a sort of bastardized, simplistic English, perhaps somewhat like Esperanto. This widely held view fed into oralists' arguments that English, both written and spoken, was innately superior to ASL. Although Stokoe had no previous experience with the Deaf community, his linguistic background in Middle English allowed him to take a fresh and unique look at the language he was immersed in at Gallaudet, where signing was the first—and only—language of all the students and most of the faculty. What he discovered right in front of him changed the course of deaf history. As Jane Maher wrote in *Seeing Language in Sign*,

He was the first to look for a structure, to analyze signs, to dissect them, to search for constituent parts.... He delineated nineteen different handshapes, twelve locations, and twenty-four types of movements. These symbols, moreover, were linked in a syntax or grammar every bit as complex and complete as that of spoken language. In 1960, he published his groundbreaking paper, "Sign Language Structure," and five years later... the monumental *Dictionary of American Sign Language on Linguistic Principles*.[1]

Moreover, Stokoe made the "first crack in the dam that eventually erupted into the flood of what we call deaf empowerment."[2] The argument is that without a legitimately recognized language, there could be no culture or self-identity. Without those, the Deaf community was always in a "one down" position, with the "hearing" majority continuing to successfully push their own judgments upon the deaf.

In retrospect, the interesting thing about the work of Stokoe was that he received virtually no support from either his colleagues or the students. If he had not been both hired and supported by the president of Gallaudet, Leonard M. Elstad, a friend from college, he may have been fired or simply consigned to oblivion. Now, however, the Deaf community is openly grateful for his work. Maher summarizes, "Bill didn't just discover a language; he laid the foundation of most of what's happened to empower deaf people and gain them the access they deserve."[3]

His work led to what happened on March 6, 1998. There were a few candidates for the vacant office of president, several of them deaf. Yet the board selected Elisabeth Zinser, the sole hearing candidate. The reaction was outraged disbelief. At a meeting at the Mayflower Hotel, where the board had been staying, the students claimed that Zinser (who has steadfastly denied it) proclaimed loudly and with conviction that deaf people were not able to function in a hearing world. That did it. Protestors shut down the campus for the next thirty-five days. The protestors, supported by faculty and staff, issued four demands:

1. That a new deaf president be named immediately.
2. That Jane Bassett Spilman, chair of the board of trustees (who, it was alleged, announced the board's choice with the comment that "the deaf are not yet ready to function in the hearing world") resign immediately.
3. That the board of trustees, at that time composed of seventeen hearing members and four deaf, be reconstituted with a 51 percent majority of deaf members.
4. That there would be no reprisals.

And so it was. Another candidate, I. King Jordan, a popular faculty member who had become deaf at the age of twenty-one in a motorcycle accident, was appointed president, and a majority of the board was theretofore to be deaf. The deaf had found their voice, their power, and their place to stand proud.

Notes

[1] Jane Maher, *Seeing Language in Sign: The Work of William C. Stokoe* (Washington, DC: Gallaudet University Press, 1996).
[2] Ibid.
[3] Ibid.

Chapter 13
Current Educational, Medical, and Legal Issues: Who Decides for the Deaf

In 1990, President George H. W. Bush signed the Americans with Disabilities Act. It included both the Deaf community and those with hearing loss. When I became deaf in May 2008, I knew this act should cover me. I was a graduate student at Pacific School of Religion, an interdenominational seminary in Berkeley, California, and enrolled in a "Sexuality and Spirituality" certificate (my required fifteen-page paper turned into the first edition of this book, at a whopping 146 pages), but obviously I could not continue my education without hearing remedies.

My partner and I went to speak with the dean of students. Well, I spoke, but the dean had to write her responses. She immediately agreed to hire a CART (Communication Access Realtime Translation) captioner who would go to all my classes, sitting next to me with her computer while typing out what the instructor and my classmates were saying. She even transcribed Sheryl's and my legal wedding in the Disciples of Christ chapel on the campus, with an American Baptist gay clergyman. When it came time to say our vows, she went up to the altar with us so I could know what words were said. She refused to take any money for it. Bless her!

Then, as we finally found out how the hearing loop works (putting down copper wiring on the floor, ceiling, or under the floor, which then connected to an amplifier plugged in to the main amplifier), the situation got a bit more complex. Fortunately, Sheryl had been the first female engineer ever hired by Kellogg's main plant in Omaha before she experienced a calling to ministry, so, once she heard my excitement when I got to use my telecoil at a lecture at the San Leandro office of deaf services, she actively pursued the hearing loop at the Pacific chapel. As soon as she grasped the concept, we boldly went to the IT office on campus. Of course, none of them had even heard of hearing loops. Probably the one at the deaf office in San Leandro was the only hearing loop at that time in all of California.

Sheryl was usually gone on Thursdays for her Clinical Pastoral Education unit at the VA unit in Sacramento, so she was puzzled during her first Thursday attendance after they had installed the loop. The IT workers did not know that the wire could be welded to another wire, so, by the time they had connected the amplifier and copper wiring to the main amplifier in a side room, they had just enough wire to loop the first part of the first pew closest to the audio room. Sheryl was quite surprised when I marched up to that seat for the next service. Unless I am doing something in the service, I prefer sitting in the back row towards the exit. She soon taught the IT staff how to extend loops, and finally I could sit anywhere in the chapel and resumed my place in the back.

Later, after we had both graduated and moved to Iowa in 2009, Sheryl flew out from Omaha to attend the Earl lectures and found out that the loop was not working. The IT employee said to her, "Oh, is Mary with you?" In retrospect, it is almost funny. It is a gradual and slow learning curve, it seems, for those with no hearing loss!

Fast-forward to 2016. When I was serving on the Deaf Services Commission of Iowa from 2015 to 2019, even our usual meeting room was not looped. The state capitol itself, even its legislative chambers, was using an inadequate FM system to comply with the ADA law. This doesn't work well because FM systems only make the sound louder, and each individual has to have a headset, so someone has to check them out, check them back in, clean them for the next users, and recharge them. After a lot of research and communication with people from other states who were able to get laws enacted for hearing loops in their chambers and other public places, with the expert help of Stephen Frazier, an attorney from Albuquerque, New Mexico, I drafted a bill that would require an audiologist or hearing instrument specialist to inform their clients about telecoils and hearing loops and have this in writing for them to study.

I contacted a state house legislator, Art Staed, from Cedar Rapids, 284 miles away, to meet with him at his home. It took us five hours to get there. He and his wife welcomed us warmly. After speaking with him about the legislation (which would cost nothing and could only be acted on if a client reported an audiologist or hearing loss specialist who had not complied), we drove the long way back home. By the time we had reached it, Art had already submitted the hearing access bill. Yet in the Republican-controlled subcommittee the bill never made it to the floor for a vote. My obvious and logical conclusion was that Republicans do not suffer hearing loss the way Democrats and Independents do.

There are many interlaced issues concerning the Deaf community in regard to education and medical and legal issues, all worthy of much more space than can be allotted in this book. I do wish, however, to write briefly about some particularly cogent and pressing issues. Among them are the Americans with Disabilities Act; bilingualism and the ADA, particularly in regard to the needs of deaf children; the concomitant earlier enactment of PL 94-142, which mandated appropriate public education of virtually all children; and the advent and extension of cochlear implants and their impact on the Deaf community.

The Americans with Disabilities Act of 1990

One would think that the Deaf community, by and large, would have welcomed the 1990 Americans with Disabilities Act with open arms. Not so. In fact, a large majority of the Deaf community (here, again, I reiterate that I am speaking of those born and culturally deaf, not hard-of-hearing or late-deafened, as I am) has many issues with it. Two years earlier, in 1988, with the success of the "Deaf President Now" protest at Gallaudet University, the deaf had taken the world stage with the message of their right to live, learn, and work as competent adults, side by side with and equal to the hearing society. Part of this "coming of age" was to eschew the label of "disabled." This was a prevalent, long-standing attitude among the deaf.

In fact, in 1945, Byron B. Byrnes, president of the National Association of the Deaf, appeared before a senate committee considering an extra income tax exemption for deaf people, just as it had already been granted to the blind. Jerome Schein writes, "He argued that Deaf people did not want to be singled out; they preferred improved education that would enable them to compete equally, rather than to appear before the public as less capable than others."[1] Yet again, in an irony that undetected by most of the audist establishment, the deaf were included as "disabled," continuing now in national law a perception long held and still, to a large part, practiced by the medical establishment (see the section below on cochlear implants and children).

It has certainly been helpful to have federal laws surrounding employment and communications access that mandate reasonable accommodation for those who are hard-of-hearing or deaf, and much more is needed in that regard. Large segments of society are "deaf" to the communication needs of the deaf, late-deafened, and hard-of-hearing, with communities of faith and seminaries near the top of the list (and, just as difficult for me personally, most movie theaters!). Yet do the deaf have to be labeled "disabled," with all the attendant prejudice and discrimination that go hand in hand with it? This is an intriguing question, posed here merely rhetorically but worthy of further discussion.

Bilingualism and Public Education

Like the ADA Act, this is a complex issue. Before discussing the federal law, it bears repeating that the work of William Stokoe on the linguistic structure of ASL ultimately convinced even his most rigorous critics, the deaf foremost among them (another example of horizontal oppression perhaps?), that American Sign Language was a language in its own right, thus taking its legitimate place among others such as French, English, and Spanish. One need only glance through a number of college catalogues to find that ASL can be used to fulfill the language requirements for graduation.

Despite William Stokoe's groundbreaking, yet not initially supported, work in going against assumptions held as doctrine by both the hearing and deaf communities and showing that American Sign Language is truly a language in *all* aspects, not just a bastardized, reductionist manual expression of written or spoken English, when the law about bilingual education was enacted, it did not and still does not apply to students whose native language is sign. In brief, the Bilingual Education Act of 1968, otherwise known as Title VII of the Elementary and Secondary Education Act, basically transformed the way language-minority children were to be taught in the United States—by promoting equal access to the curriculum, training educators, and fostering achievement among students. Ironically, despite the work of Stokoe and the acceptance of ASL as fulfilling foreign language requirements on many university campuses, this act did not seem to extend to deaf children whose primary or sole language was ASL.

In some ways, the issue right now is "dead." The source article for this information was titled "The Bilingual Education Act 1968–2002: An Obituary."[2] Fueled by xenophobic right-wingers under the innocuous title of "No Child Left Behind," the act was proposed by the Bush administration but passed with broad bipartisan support. Without fanfare, the Bilingual Education Act became the English Language Acquisition Act (Title III). As Crawford reveals, not a single member of the Congressional Hispanic Caucus, once a stalwart ally of Title VII, voted against the legislation. This is particularly ironic, as large numbers of non-English-speaking citizens, indeed, voters, are changing the American political landscape.

The goal of the English Language Acquisition Act is to make it mandatory for non-English-speaking children to learn English—as fast as possible. On the surface, this looks like a good idea, but again it highlights xenophobia and contradicts the real evidence of many other countries that do not have one dominant language being able to have a cohesive society and transact laws. And this act, too, fails to understand the underlying fundamental difference between any spoken language and the language of the deaf, which is both manual and visible.

Voices of opposition to this monolingual approach are not hard to find. Harlan Lane declares that "Deaf children who do best in school, mainstream or residential, are—note it well—the fortunate 10 percent who learned ASL as a native language from their deaf parents, the core of this linguistic minority."[3] He is joined by a UNESCO report:

> A few years ago, UNESCO called in consultants on deaf education from around the globe to advise it on the different approaches to the education of deaf children. The UNESCO report concludes that deaf adults have an important role to play "in the development and education of deaf children" and finds that the interaction of deaf adults with the parents, the deaf children and the teachers also "enriches the socialization of the deaf child."[4]

Mainstreaming and Public Law 94-142

In 1975, Public Law 94-142 (Education of All Handicapped Children Act) was enacted. On the surface, this, too, sounded promising. Its goal was to provide free appropriate public education to all children with disabilities, and it explicitly included deaf children. This meant that a child following an IEP, or Individualized Education Program, was to be placed in the "least restrictive environment." For many children, this meant taking them out of a "warehousing" environment and mainstreaming them as efficiently and quickly as possible, with a learning resource center providing ancillary support.[5]

In addition, the Deaf Education Options Guide, specifically the section on public laws affecting deaf education, outlines how federal laws like the Individuals with Disabilities Education Act (IDEA) and the Americans with Disabilities Act (ADA) ensure equal access to education and services for Deaf students. These laws require schools to provide a "free appropriate public education" and accommodations, including interpreters and assistive technology, to meet the individual needs of Deaf students.

The Individuals with Disabilities Education Act (IDEA), Section 504 of the Rehabilitation Act, and the Americans with Disabilities Act (ADA) are key federal laws that impact deaf education. These laws ensure equal access to education, employment, and public services for individuals with disabilities, including deaf individuals. They provide frameworks for accommodations and address issues like effective communication and the "interactive process" in accommodation decision-making.

Then, in 1986, Public Law 94-142 was further amended by Public Law 99-457 (Education of the Handicapped Amendments of 1986). Finally, the 1990 Individuals with Disabilities Education Act (IDEA) was enacted. The IDEA now refers to the entire package of laws that assures a decent public education for all children with disabilities. IDEA sounds great on paper. It requires an early and unbiased evaluation of hearing loss in school-age children and an unbiased evaluation of deaf children using a variety of communication methods, including sign language. It even requires that tests and other evaluation materials used to assess a child are provided and administered in the child's native language or other mode of communication unless it is clearly not feasible to do so.

What has happened in reality, time and time again, is that a deaf child is placed in an LRE (Least Restrictive Environment) as the only deaf child, isolated from peers, frequently having to rely on an inadequately trained interpreter, with neither the other students nor the teacher being at all conversant with sign. Obviously, to an audist system, having a deaf child placed in a hearing classroom with hearing peers is somehow supposed to be a gain, a privilege, something that both the deaf child and parents would clearly want. The audist "mask of benevolence" strikes again.

Cochlear Implants

This section is extraordinarily difficult to write about, not only because of its complexity but also because it reveals in such a stark way the main place where the audist community and the Deaf community are having the most heated discussions. An in-depth study of cochlear implants, not just the medical nuts and bolts of the diagnosis and surgery but the positions people take around the issue, would be adequate to give someone an encapsulated version of the main "colonial" assumptions about the "subjugated" population of both the Deaf and LGBT communities.

The first order of business is to describe a cochlear implant. Approved for use in United States in 1990, although it had been the first choice for assistive listening in western Europe for decades, it involves diagnosing a profound and irremediable hearing loss, then a surgery whereby the damaged parts of the inner ear are bypassed, and a thin wire connected to the auditory nerve is inserted into the cochlea. A surgically inserted implant behind the ear and attached to the wire is then connected through a magnet to an outer sound processor, allowing a deaf person to hear sounds again. The timing of the hearing loss, whether one was pre- or post-lingual when it happened, and the recentness of intelligible speech all have an impact on how much and how well the implanted person can understand speech.

What could be the problem with this procedure? The main problem is that the implant age kept getting pushed back from an adult cognizant of the risks and benefits and making a personal decision to a pre-lingual child and now, even a baby. While the cochlear implant has a high degree of success medically, it is still a major surgical intervention with concomitant risks such as meningitis, other infections, and failure.

The question is not only who makes the decision for this surgery but also how they are "primed" to make a decision. With deaf parents, having a deaf child is almost uniformly seen as a blessing, even desired over a hearing child. But more than 90 percent of deaf children are born to hearing parents, so we must look beneath the social constructs of the audist establishment to revisit in more detail the medical and social models that would unilaterally and unequivocally favor a cochlear implant, no questions asked. In his groundbreaking book, *Theology without Words: Theology in the Deaf Community*,[6] Wayne Morris spends a great deal of time discussing issues such as these before launching specifically into deaf theology.

The medical model is based on seeing deafness as an impairment or handicap or disability—as simply a fixable lack of hearing, which is viewed as something negative. Therefore, anything that can "correct" this is good. For physicians, the technology of the cochlear implant is an answer to "prayer." There is thus no discussion of the deaf child's social context, no exploration of the child's support system, and no encouragement for the parents to acknowledge the child's deafness by linking to the Deaf community, history, or culture. Cochlear implants become a quick fix. As Morris explains,

> The medical model's goal is one in which it is assumed to be ethically right that the Deaf child is enabled to be as much like a hearing child as possible. ...Playing on those parents' fears of "abnormality" and their desire to achieve "normality", they [proponents of the medical approach] then present their medical model which claims that normality can only be achieved by denying the realities of deafness and keeping their children away from Deaf communities lest they be "contaminated" by them.[7]

The social model is a bit less sinister on the surface. It ascribes to the belief that the "blame" for the disability cannot be placed on the affected person, but society must do everything possible to remove social and environmental barriers to full participation in the larger, "non-disabled" society. Their goal of "normality" for all disabled people, while perhaps coming from a sense of generosity and even justice, is still weighted to a narrow understanding of what "normal" is. Work done by disabled people and the World Health Organization posits a new approach that addresses the above concerns and offers a fresh model. This approach involves respecting disabled people as unique human beings with gifts and abilities. It accepts that social barriers suppress the ability of many disabled people to participate fully in society and recognizes that medical intervention can be useful for many disabled people, provided it is not imposed on disabled people. Choice and freedom are paramount. This new approach also recognizes that disabled people are a diverse group, and no single model is realistically applicable to all.

What does the debate look like within the Deaf community? If we are willing to let go of our audist assumptions and prerogatives, how has the Deaf community been handling the ready availability of cochlear implant technology? Years ago, the battle lines were drawn. It was, as it were, a Maginot line of intractable doctrine with the deaf on one side and the audist establishment on the other. Yet, in the last few years, there has been a major tectonic shift in such entrenched positions. Michael Chorost wrote about reactions at Gallaudet:

> In 1993, student protests had led to the cancellation of a forum on cochlear implants at Gallaudet University, the United States' flagship university for the signing deaf. In 2000, however, 59 percent of Gallaudet's faculty, staff, and students questioned in a poll agreed that the school should do

more to encourage students with cochlear implants to attend. Gallaudet now has a center devoted to supporting students with cochlear implants.[8]

Then he wrote about the National Association of the Deaf, which heretofore had been adamantly, across the board, opposed to lowering the age for cochlear implants for children, going so far as to accuse the medical establishment of conspiring to commit "cultural genocide."[9] "Now," Chorost said, "the NAD recognizes the rights of parents to make informed choices for their deaf and hard-of-hearing children, respects their choice to use cochlear implants and all other assistive devices, and strongly supports the development of the whole child and of language and literacy."[10]

Ironically, when Chorost met with Philip Aiello, who had chaired the NAD's committee for revising its position paper on cochlear implants in 2000, Aiello was sporting a cochlear implant. Chorost went on to state, "It had taken the NAD two full years of passionate argument to draft its new position statement, and its ethic of tolerance and open-mindedness is doubtless due in no small part to his [Aiello's] leadership."[11] The "Position Statement on Early Cognitive and Language Development and Education" goes into much more detail:

> Hearing aids have been acceptable and effective listening devices and cochlear implants can, in some cases, be important in the development of spoken English. However, these technologies and devices vary greatly in their linguistic benefit to individual deaf and hard of hearing children. …[I]nformed estimates indicate that no more than 40 percent of deaf and hard of hearing children who have cochlear implants but do not use sign language get a linguistic benefit from the device. …Reliance on only spoken language input via cochlear implants may result in linguistic deprivation if sign language is excluded from the environment of the child. Put simply, if the child is only provided linguistic input through speech and hearing and the CI does not provide the child clear and unambiguous access to this input, language learning is compromised.[12]

To see the personal and familial tension and conflict surrounding a child's receiving a cochlear implant, it is well worth viewing the 2000 documentary *Sound and Fury*.[13] It is about the two Artinian brothers—one deaf, the other hearing—who both have deaf children. The entire extended family, including both grandparents, was facile in sign language, so the brothers grew up in a bilingual household. The hearing brother, who had married a hearing woman, had twin boys, one deaf and the other hearing. He moved easily to the position of wanting a cochlear implant for his child as soon as possible. The deaf brother, who had married a deaf woman, had a deaf daughter of kindergarten age, Heather, who wanted a cochlear implant.

Initially opposed, the deaf brother's family did a lot of investigating, with all the hearing members of the extended family urging them to get the implant for their daughter. Instead, after seeing Heather interacting so well in a school setting with other deaf children where sign language was the predominant method of communication, they literally uprooted their family and moved to a community in another state so she could go to school there, leaving a very upset extended family in New York state.

Fast-forward to *Sound and Fury: 6 Years Later*.[14] In this short update, we learn that Heather, her two younger brothers, and her born-deaf mother have had cochlear implants. They moved back to New York to be with their extended family. Then Heather became the only deaf student in a public high school and was very active in student life, including being on the girls' basketball team. After graduating from Gallaudet University, where she worked diligently to have the school bridge the gap between the cochlear implant and deaf worlds, she went on to become a lawyer after getting her JD from Harvard Law School in 2018.[15]

Although Heather Artinian seems to have overcome a somewhat "late" implanting, in general this is tricky because the small child's brain is growing exponentially in regard to language acquisition skills, as the body itself is growing in size, strength, and coordination. Chorost noted, "There is a risk to delaying early exposure to a sign language just as there is a risk to delaying early exposure to speech for children who hear. …If a child gets to the age of four without having acquired fluent and natural diction, chances are slim that he or she ever will."[16]

And yet, as Carol Padden summarizes, "Today, the same concerns exist; there are doctors and teachers who say that they are ambivalent about the future of sign language while they are enthusiastic about the future of technology like cochlear implants."[17] Padden had the pleasure of interviewing the adult Heather Artinian, who received her cochlear implant age the age of nine years old. One of her questions was, "How has your cochlear implant made a difference in your life so far?" Heather answered, "It definitely changed everything. I came from being solely in the deaf culture, to being in both. I learned how to communicate with hearing people. I was able to take on leadership positions at school, well- because of the CI, I was able to go to a hearing [school] district. I'm more prepared to take on the hearing world. I feel as if I am deaf, and a hearing person."[18]

It is yet to be established if she will become a Supreme Court Justice. Personally, I hope so.

A "Final Solution" for Deafness?

With the lines softening around cochlear implants and more people who are born deaf getting them at younger ages, it seems that the number of those who are deaf without access to sophisticated hearing technology will continue growing smaller. In addition, we now have major advances in genetic engineering, mapping the human genome, and amniocentesis, where parents can get a detailed reading of the fetus's genetic disposition before birth. While some deafness comes about by chance, sickness, or accident, there are families who carry a "deaf" gene. This could theoretically mean that someone could abort a fetus who is deaf solely because it is deaf.

The main question is how society views deafness. With a medical model, both Doctors and scientists are approaching a time when they can both identify and "correct" genetic deafness, which might lead to the elimination of deaf communities and sign languages.

Carol Padden claims, in no uncertain terms,

> Genetic engineering has as its goal not the preservation of sign language, but the elimination of deafness so that no child will be consigned to using sign language. The popular media continue to write stories about children with cochlear implants who achieve the ability to hear and use speech, implying directly or indirectly that the child does not need sign language anymore because he or she has the possibility of speech.[19]

Padden concludes with a clarion cry that must be heeded: "Deaf people today face the most important challenge of voice: How do they voice their concerns at a time when medical technologies and genetic engineering have stated their goal as the elimination of deafness?"

The Passing of a Culture

There is, as noted above, a real possibility that the Deaf community as it is constituted now will be a culture of the past rather than a living, vibrant, and unique addition to our common humanity, but its passing will at great cost. Michael Chorost, visiting the Deaf school that he had attended and seeing so many young children with cochlear implants, stated, "What I felt was joy: joy at the opening of human potential, at the destruction of barriers, at the flowering of lives that might have been limited and shuttered. For profound deafness to be rendered ultimately a nuisance—surely that was occasion for tears of pride and gratitude."[20] Yet this brought about a concomitant sorrow. He wrote about a young woman named Jessica, whom he had just interviewed after she received a cochlear implant:

This *is* the world that Jessica is inheriting. Instead of becoming more like the signing deaf community, American life is becoming steadily less like it, ever more atomized and isolated. Because of the implant, she now has access to a larger world, and the immense significance of that gift cannot be denied, but it is also a colder world. It is a world in which she may have more academic degrees and more money, but fewer friends.[21]

Notes

[1] Jerome D. Schein, *At Home Among Strangers: Exploring the Deaf Community in the United States* (Washington, DC: Gallaudet University Press, 1998), 26.

[2] James Crawford, "The Bilingual Education Act 1968–2002," 2008, http://www.languagepolicy.net/books/AEL/Crawford_BEA_Obituary.pdf.

[3] Harlan Lane, *The Mask of Benevolence: Disabling the Deaf Community* (San Diego, CA: DawnSign Press, 1999), 138.

[4] Ibid., 166.

[5] See "Deaf Students Education Services," *U.S. Department of Education*, https://www.ed.gov/about/offices/list/ocr/docs/hq9806.html.

[6] Wayne Morris, *Theology without Words: Theology in the Deaf Community* (Hampshire, England: Ashgate Publishing Limited, 2008).

[7] Ibid., 8, 9.

[8] Michael Chorost, *Rebuilt: My Journey Back to the Hearing World* (USA: Mariner Books, 2005), 132.

[9] Ibid., 130.

[10] Ibid., 133.

[11] Ibid., 134.

[12] "Position Statement on Early Cognitive and Language Development and Education of Deaf and Hard of Hearing Children," *National Association of the Deaf*, https://www.nad.org/about-us/position-statements/position-statement-on-early-cognitive-and-language-development-and-education-of-deaf-and-hard-of-hearing-children/.

[13] *Sound and Fury*, directed by Josh Aronson, Artistic License Films, 80 minutes, 2000.

[14] Also directed by Josh Aronson, Aronson Films, 29 minutes, 2006.

[15] Lewis Rice, "Heather Artinian '18," *Harvard Law Today*, May 10, 2018, https://hls.harvard.edu/today/heather-artinian-18-people-tell-no-just-becomes-motivator/.

[16] Chorost, *Rebuilt*, 29.

[17] Carol Padden and Tom Humphries, *Inside Deaf Culture* (Cambridge, MA: Harvard University Press, 2005), 161.

[18] Ibid.

[19] Ibid.

[20] Chorost, *Rebuilt*, quoted in Jennifer Durgin, "Sound and Silence," *Dartmouth Medicine*, Fall 2008.

[21] Ibid.

Chapter 14

Current Educational, Medical, and Legal Issues: Who Decides for LGBT?

As with the Deaf community, there are several issues for the LGBT community. I will discuss the changing stances of the American Psychiatric Association and their sister organization, the American Psychological Association, regarding the diagnosis and treatment of homosexuality following the Stonewall Riots; issues of discrimination and hate legislation; the status of AIDS; educational issues and magnet schools; and, only briefly, the military and then marriage (discussed further under the "Queer Theology" section).

Changing Stance of the American Psychiatric Association

This change relates to the diagnosis of homosexuality as a disorder. In 1970, gay activists entered the American Psychiatric Association's annual conference, specifically a workshop on aversion therapy, which led to the APA reevaluating its stance on homosexuality. With the weight of empirical data, coupled with changing societal norms, in 1973 the Board of Directors removed homosexuality from the Diagnostic and Statistical Manual. Some psychiatrists who fiercely opposed this action circulated a petition calling for a vote on the issue by the association's membership. The vote, in 1974, upheld the board's decision.

The DSM-III, issued in 1980, included a new diagnosis, "ego-dystonic homosexuality," which was to be given to someone who was significantly distressed by homosexual feelings or actions. Many viewed this as a bone thrown to psychiatrists who did not want homosexuality removed as a diagnostic category, but others thought it did not go far enough in removing homosexuality altogether as a mental illness. Thus, in 1986, the diagnosis was finally removed entirely as a classification. In 1975, the American Psychological Association followed close on the heels of the American Psychiatric Association in also getting rid of the "homosexuality" diagnosis. The trend continued in the current DSM V edition, published in 2013. There are simply no longer diagnostic categories that can be applied to people based on their homosexual orientation. (It is not within the scope of this book to discuss transgender issues and gender dysphoria, though I suspect research would show similar changes in perspectives over time.)

Continued Opposition

The opposition, of course, didn't disappear. Several die-hard psychiatrists, psychologists, and other health professionals still hold that homosexuality is a major disorder. Many so-called religious people find their rallying cry around calling for death to homosexuals. Many so-called experts address the "homosexual agenda." The results of the 2024 presidential election have added fuel to the previously dying embers.

Possibly the biggest "player" in the campaign to reinstitute homosexuality as a mental illness was Charles Socarides (1922–2005), who throughout his life adamantly resisted changing public or mental health attitudes towards homosexuality. Up to his death he maintained that homosexuality could be altered. To this end he founded the National Association for Research and Therapy of Homosexuality (NARTH) in 1992 (the association disbanded in 2014). While he did not consider homosexuality a moral failure, he viewed it as something that could be remedied by appropriate therapy.

The mission of NARTH sounded benign and respectful:

> We respect the right of all individuals to choose their own destiny. NARTH is a professional, scientific organization that offers hope to those who struggle with unwanted homosexuality. As an organization, we disseminate educational information, conduct and collect scientific research, promote effective therapeutic treatment, and provide referrals to those who seek our assistance. NARTH upholds the rights of individuals with unwanted homosexual attraction to receive effective psychological care and the right of professionals to offer that care. We welcome the participation of all individuals who will join us in the pursuit of these goals.[1]

While believing that clients had the right to claim a gay identity, NARTH also believed that it was their right to diminish their homosexuality and develop their heterosexual potential. Of course, this begs the question, how much of one's desire to change one's sexual orientation relates to the very real costs—familial, professional, self-esteem—caused by homophobia?

Exodus International, founded in 1976, was like NARTH, although a bit more aggressive and a lot more religious: "Exodus is a nonprofit, interdenominational Christian organization promoting the message of Freedom from homosexuality through the power of Jesus Christ."[2] Since 1976, Exodus had grown to include more than 230 local ministries in the USA and Canada and was also linked with other Exodus world regions outside of North America through the Exodus Global Alliance. "Within both the Christian and secular communities," the former webpage touted, "Exodus has challenged those who respond to homosexuals with ignorance and fear, and those who uphold homosexuality as a valid orientation. These extremes fail to convey the fullness of redemption found in Jesus Christ, a gift which is available to all who commit their life and their sexuality to Him." In 2006, Exodus International had more than 250 local ministries in the United States and Canada and more than 150 ministries in 17 other countries. Although Exodus was formally an interdenominational Christian entity, it was most closely associated with Protestant and evangelical denominations.

In 2012, Alan Chambers, then president of the group, renounced conversion therapy, saying it did not work and was harmful. The following year, Chambers closed the organization and apologized for the "pain and hurt" participants of their programs had experienced. Several other prominent former members, including John Paulk, have made similar apologies.[3] While Exodus International no longer operates, many of its member ministries continue to do so, either forming new networks, joining existing ones such as the Exodus Global Alliance, or operating independently. Apokata Psychological Services ("apokata" means "restoration") in San Francisco is affiliated with Exodus International. Their professional staff are certified by the state of California, despite, it seems, their opposition to the American Psychiatric Association's and American Psychological Association's thirty-year-plus stances on homosexuality.

There are also people whose lives revolve around their absolute hatred of homosexuals. A case in point is Fred Phelps (1929–2014), who hailed from Topeka, Kansas. His mission was to stage anti-gay protests all over the country. In addition, there are generic, anonymous hatemongers on the internet, where I went to find out what people think is the "homosexual agenda." According to the Conservapedia (an online encyclopedia written from a self-described American conservative and fundamentalist Christian point of view),[4]

> One of the top priorities of the Homosexual Agenda is to prohibit and outlaw conversion therapy. Activities like baseball and chess reduce homosexual proclivities, while other activities like figure skating for men and soccer for women seem to encourage homosexuality. Leftists are pushing unconstitutional bans on conversion therapy, apparently unable to tolerate things they dislike. Their priorities include electing high-ranking officials who are openly homosexual, with the ultimate goal of electing a president who is in a same-sex marriage, like the top Dem fundraising candidate Pete Buttigieg in 2020.

The site goes on to include a list that they say defines the homosexual agenda:

- Legalize homosexuality
- Hold "gay pride" parades

- Accept child sex trafficking
- Demand non-discrimination laws
- Insist on homosexuals' adoption of children
- Push the homosexual agenda in schools
- Legalize various alternate forms of partnership and call them "marriage" (i.e. man and man, woman and woman, man and multiple women)
- Demand public funding to deal with increased homosexual-related social problems
- Promote the gender confusion agenda
- Demand to be treated "equally"
- Impose a large-scale loss of free speech
- Ban counseling for kids confused by homosexual issues
- Drag queen story times to indoctrinate children
- Ban scientifically and religiously proven methods of homosexual conversion
- Attack churches
- Encourage abortion

Reading this list made me contemplate what my "homosexual agenda" was for today. Feed all ten of my animals. Take my meds. Walk the dog. Working on editing. Pray the lectionary with my *female* spouse (oh, no!). Watch *Highway to Heaven* at lunchtime. Nap with my two cuddle cats, Priscilla and Bart, do more editing, prune bushes outside, read a mystery novel, then become a couch potato in front of the TV all evening. I hope this agenda does not offend anyone!

Current Status of Discrimination and Hate Legislation

Until the end of Barack Obama's presidency in 2017, there was heartening, even amazing progress in many areas. The Matthew Shepard and James Byrd Jr. Hate Crimes Prevention Act was enacted in 2009. Matthew was an American student at the University of Wyoming who was beaten, tortured, and left to die on October 12, 1998, by two other students simply because he was a gay young man. This was a turning point for gay rights in the United States, prompting outrage, sorrow, and activism. His killers were both given consecutive life sentences, although they weren't charged with a hate crime.

> In order to avoid the death penalty, Henderson (one of his two killers) pleads guilty to murder and kidnapping charges. At a court hearing, Henderson tells Shepard's parents "I regret greatly what I did." Henderson was sentenced to two consecutive life terms, making the possibility of parole

unlikely. Henderson, said, "I think about Matthew every single day of my life. I think about him and every single one of those days that I've had that he hasn't had, his family hasn't had, his friends haven't had. I'm so, so ashamed I was ever part of this."[5]

A cross marks the area where he was beaten and left tied to a fence shortly after midnight on October 7, 1998, in Laramie. He died in a Colorado hospital a week later. The fence has since been torn down. Shepard's story is depicted in 2002's *The Matthew Shepard Story*, which originally aired on NBC.[6] It can now be found on Peacock. In addition, his mother, Judy Shepard, published a memoir, *The Meaning of Matthew: My Son's Murder in Laramie, and a World Transformed*.[7]

James Byrd Jr. was an African American man lynched in 1998 by three white men—Shawn Berry, Lawrence Brewer, and John King—who dragged him for three miles behind their pickup truck along an asphalt road. After they confirmed he was dead, the murderers dumped his torso in front of a Black cemetery. Two of them, Brewer and King, became the first white men sentenced to death in Texas for killing a Black person. Berry was sentenced to life imprisonment.[8] In 2001, this horrific action led Texas to pass a hate crimes law that directly led Congress to pass the Matthew Shepard and James Byrd Jr. Hate Crimes Prevention Act in 2009.[9] This long-overdue act provides both funding and technical assistance to jurisdictions for local, state, and even tribal jurisdictions to help them both investigate and prosecute hate crimes.

It is heartening that these tragic and hate-filled violent deaths, one of an African American man and another of a gay man, led to the passage of these new hate laws, but it will never make up for the horrid and tortuous deaths the two of them suffered, one for the color of his skin and the other because of his sexual orientation.

The Changing Moral Landscape of Major Protestant Churches

In churches, LGBT inclusion varies greatly, not only in pastoral theology but also in issues surrounding ordination. At the time of completion of my research paper leading to this book, for instance, the Disciples of Christ had no national policy but allowed a church-by-church decision.

At the General Assembly in 2013, the Christian Church (Disciples of Christ) voted to affirm and welcome LGBTQ people in all aspects of church life, including leadership. While the resolution does not dictate policy for individual congregations, the denomination actively encourages congregations interested in becoming more inclusive:

The General Assembly calls upon the Church to recognize itself as striving to become a people of grace and welcome to all God's children though differing in sexual orientation or gender identity, affirming that neither are grounds for exclusion from fellowship or service within the church, and calling upon all expressions of the Christian Church (Disciples of Christ), as a people of grace and welcome, to acknowledge their support for the welcome of and hospitality to all.[10]

At that same assembly, I introduced a resolution I wrote to extend "welcoming" to include those with hearing loss. It passed by acclamation. It was a big year! In addition to calling on the General Assembly and regions to make meetings fully accessible to those with hearing loss, the submitters called for a workshop at the 2015 assembly on how groups were implementing these strategies.[11]

In 2015, the church spoke out against Indiana's Religious Freedom Restoration Act, which allows discrimination against LGBTQ consumers. Currently, the United Church of Christ, the Presbyterian Church (PCUSA), the Episcopalian Church in the US, the Evangelical Lutheran Church of America, the Unitarians (UUA), the Christian Church (Disciples of Christ, of which I am a clergywoman), American Baptists, United Methodist Church, and the CRC (Reformed Church of Christ) welcome full inclusion of LGBT people, including being ordained. In the denominations with congregational models, it is up to an individual church to make that decision. The Methodist Church has been torn apart for years on this issue, with a permanent split over this issue finally happening in 2024.

In 1974, three bishops from the American Episcopal Church ordained eleven women deacons to the priesthood in Philadelphia, a move that was considered irregular by the church's canons. This act, though controversial, brought the issue of women's ordination into greater focus and highlighted the existing divisions within the church. The three prophetic bishops were Daniel Corrigan, Robert L. DeWitt, and Edward R. Welles II. They conducted the ordinations at the Church of the Advocate in Philadelphia on July 29, 1974, making these women the first female priests in the Episcopal Church. In 1976, The General Convention formally approved the ordination of women both to the priesthood and episcopate in 1976. The names of the "Philadelphia Eleven" should not be forgotten: Merrill Bittner, Alla Bozarth-Campbell, Alison Cheek, Emily Hewitt, Carter Heyward, Suzanne Hiatt, Marie Moorefield, Jeannette Piccard, Betty Bone Schiess, Katrina Swanson, and Nancy Wittig. Carter Heyward's *Our Passion for Justice* (1984), became a big part of my own faith journey as I sought to find my own place in a faith community that would fully support the gifts I had been given.

As I was updating and cross-checking this manuscript, I stumbled upon a more recent call to action in her recent book, *The Seven Deadly Sins of White*

Christian Nationalism: A Call to Action. In the description of her book on Amazon Prime, this analysis is well worth reading:

> Heyward shows how American Christians have played a major role in building and securing structures of injustice in American life. Rising tides of white supremacy, threats to women's reproductive freedoms and to basic human rights for gender and sexual minorities, the widening divide between rich and poor, and increasing natural disasters and the extinction of Earth's species—all point to a world crying out for God's wisdom.
>
> Followers of Jesus must first call out these ingrained and sinful attitudes for what they are, acknowledging what the culture of white Christian nationalism is doing to our country and our world, and commit ourselves ever more fully to generating justice-love, whoever and wherever we are.[12]

For the Episcopal Church in America, things moved forward fast after the barriers came down. Let me introduce you to Reverend Katherine Jefferts Shori. Jefferts Schori attended school in New Jersey, then earned a Bachelor of Science degree in biology from Stanford University in 1974, a Master of Science degree in oceanography in 1977, and a Doctor of Philosophy degree in 1983, also in oceanography, from Oregon State University. She is an instrument-rated pilot. It looked as if her career was set. But evidently God had other plans for her that rooted her solidly on the ground, not flying the skies or plumbing ocean depths.

Jefferts Schori earned her Master of Divinity in 1994 from the Church Divinity School of the Pacific, right across the street from Pacific School of Religion, where I would be in attendance from 2006–2009. She was ordained priest that year. Afterward she became the assistant pastor at the Church of the Good Samaritan in Corvallis, Oregon, where she worked with the growing Hispanic community since, between flying, oceanography, and theology, she also somehow found the time to master Spanish.

This is where our paths crossed in person. I lived in Corvallis from 1990 to 2004, and, in addition to earning my master's degree in counseling from OSU in 1992, I decided to go through the hospice training program because of my previous experiences of working with the sick, dying, and grieving. And there she was in the flesh, teaching the spiritual part of our training. In 2001, Jefferts Schori was elected and consecrated Bishop of Nevada, where it was reported that she flew a plane to visit churches too far away for driving. Six years later, she was awarded several honorary degrees from the Church Divinity School of the Pacific Seabury-Western Theological Seminary, and Sewanee: The University of the South. She was both well known and greatly respected all over the nation.

In 2003, Jefferts Schori was prophetic enough and bold enough to vote to consent to the election of Gene Robinson, an openly gay and partnered man, a move strongly opposed by many conservative Episcopalians. Thus it was probably no surprise to most members of the Episcopal church that she was the first woman elected as a primate in the Anglican Communion. She held this position until 2015, when she chose not to ask for reappointment. During her nine-year term of office, Jefferts Schori supported same-sex relationships and the blessing of same-sex unions and civil marriages. This stance on the blessing of same-sex marriage led a number of Anglican bishops to refuse Communion from her when she was in Tanzania in 2007.

Like her predecessor, she also supported abortion rights, stating that it might be a moral tragedy, but it definitely was not the role of the government to deny its availability. In our own denomination, the Christian Church (Disciples of Christ), we appointed the first woman, Sharon Watkins, to become general minister and president in 2005. She was serving in in Bartlesville, Oklahoma, at a Disciples church when I was a student at Unity School of Ministry in Lee's Summit, Missouri. I was preaching at a small Unity church there on the last day of her ministry and participated in her farewell departure. It was not until the next year, following the urging of my now-spouse, Sheryl Butler, that I became a disciple of Christ, where I still serve.

In 2017, the Christian Church (Disciples of Christ), the UCC's partner in Global Ministries, elected a new general minister and president, the Rev. Teresa "Terri" Hord Owens, to serve as the denomination's leader in the United States and Canada. She is the first African American to hold this post and the second woman to lead the Disciples of Christ. I have met Owens on a number of occasions, having several opportunities to share with her about the virtual exclusion of people with hearing loss from full communion with the church. As I already noted, a resolution regarding this issue was later passed at the General Assembly.

Status of Several Other Protestant Churches

Delegates of Mennonite Church USA voted to officially allow pastors to perform same-sex marriages, as well as apologize for the harm caused by past policies. …Two measures were voted upon at the denomination conference in Kansas City, Mo. The first vote struck down a 20-year-old document called Membership Guidelines that described "homosexual, extramarital and premarital sexual activity as sin to be the teaching position of Mennonite Church USA." That vote passed 404-84.

The second vote approved a "Repentance and Transformation" resolution that defines the harm caused by previous policies as violence, affirms the rights of LGBTQ+ members of the church and commits to further action. The vote passed with a slimmer margin of 267-212....

The announcement was also applauded by other Central Pa. LGBTQ+ organizations, such as Rainbow Rose Center in York. "We don't expect everyone to get on the same page right away. This is a process, and we applaud them for making this effort," said Tesla Taliaferro, president of the center....[13]

Several Protestant denominations are actively affirming and inclusive of LGBTQ+ individuals, providing full rights and welcoming them into leadership and ministry roles. Some notable examples include the Metropolitan Community Church, the Presbyterian Church (USA), the United Church of Christ, the Episcopal Church, the Evangelical Lutheran Church in America, the Unitarian Universalist Association, and the Christian Church (Disciples of Christ). As already noted, this hot debate within the United Methodist Church ended in a schism due to many of their churches disaffiliating with the UMC over this single issue to form their own church. They now call themselves the Global Methodist Church.

SCOTUS Decision, June 26, 2015

Probably the biggest news that year was the SCOTUS decision on June 26, 2015, that grants LGBT people the right to civil marriage, preempting the state-by-state exclusion that was currently in place. The Court voted 5–4 in *Obergefell v. Hodges*, 576 U.S. 644, that the fundamental right to marry is guaranteed to same-sex couples by both the Due Process Clause and the Equal Protection Clause of the Fourteenth Amendment to the United States Constitution. Prior to *Obergefell*, same-sex marriage had already been established by law, court ruling, or voter initiative in thirty-six states, the District of Columbia, and Guam.

I remember June 26, 2015, well. My spouse and I were at a hearing loss conference in downtown St. Louis that day and decided to take a break, so we went outside to see people literally dancing in the streets, Pride flags everywhere, and large statues decorated with rainbow colors. We were so happy, as elders in the equal rights for LGBT movement, that we began talking with young people who had taken over the streets with their Pride flags. I told them I had gone on my first gay pride march in 1992, before some of them were even born. In a rare display of "public affection," Sheryl and I held hands for the rest of the walk. Later that day, we walked down to the courthouse where Supreme Court Chief Justice Roger Taney, on March 6, 1957, had issued the court's decision against Dred Scott in the *Dred Scott v. Sandford* case. We thought about that earlier fight for equal rights and pondered how far we had come.

Dred Scott (1799–1858) was an enslaved African American man who, along with his wife Harriet, unsuccessfully sued for freedom for themselves and their two daughters, Eliza and Lizzie. The Scotts claimed that they should be granted their freedom because Dred had lived in Illinois and the Wisconsin Territory for four years, where slavery was illegal, and laws in those jurisdictions said that slaveholders gave up their rights to slaves if they stayed for an extended period. In the landmark case, the United States Supreme Court decided 7–2 against Scott, finding that neither he nor any other person of African ancestry could claim citizenship in the United States, and therefore Scott could not bring suit in a federal court under diversity of citizenship rules. The Scotts were manumitted by a private arrangement in May 1857. Dred Scott died of tuberculosis a year later. In 1863, President Abraham Lincoln's Emancipation Proclamation nullified the decision.

The courtroom where this decision took place has been turned into a small museum, and, with no docent or other visitors around, I couldn't help myself. I climbed into Chief Justice Taney's chair to meditate on the similar paths of the deaf and gay rights movements, the Civil Rights Movement, and women's liberation. As I sat there, already married legally to my female spouse, I was thankful for the great strides women have made, from the Seneca Falls convention for women's rights in 1869, with Susan B. Anthony emerging as a determined leader, to the suffragists both in Great Britain and in the United States (1920) forcing the governments to give them the long-overdue right to vote—white women, anyway. The Equal Rights Movement had stalled at the beginning line, but there were murmurs of reviving and passing it. As a final act of irony, Dred Scott's wife Harriet was never mentioned in the court decision. It was still a man's world (meaning, of course, at this time, a "white man's world"). Even so, progress had begun.

But fast-forward to 2022. SCOTUS, by a 5–4 margin, nullified *Roe v. Wade*, the 1973 Supreme Court decision that legalized abortion. Clinics are shutting down. States are now passing legislation to raise penalties for those seeking abortion, including prison for both them and abortion providers. The mayhem and destruction of this ill-considered and misogynist decision soon became clear.

A ten-year-old rape victim, six weeks pregnant, received an abortion in Indiana after being denied access in her home state of Ohio. According to *The Guardian*, the young girl's story came to public attention just three days after the overturning of *Roe v. Wade* by the Supreme Court on June 24, which pushed Ohio's six week "trigger ban" into effect.[14] Republican governor of South Dakota, Kristi Noem (now the US Secretary of Homeland Security), shared her thoughts on the ten-year-old child's situation while speaking at CNN's "State of the Union" event. Noem shared that she found it "incredible" that "nobody's talking about the pervert, horrible and deranged individual that raped a 10-year-old. As much as we talk about what we can do for that little girl, I think we also need to be addressing those sick individuals that do this to our children," she said. "What I would say is," she continued, "I don't believe a tragic situation should be perpetuated by another tragedy. And so, there's more that we have got to do to make sure that we really are living a life that says every life is precious, especially innocent lives that have been shattered, like that 10-year-old girl."[15] According to the article in *The Guardian*, abortions are now a "criminal act" in South Dakota. Rape and incest are no exception under the current South Dakota law.

Educational Issues and Magnet Schools

As with other issues, those surrounding education are complicated, so this section is illustrative rather than exhaustive. One "hot button" topic across the nation is how, where, and if information regarding sexual orientation should be included in comprehensive sex education. It is an even bigger issue currently because in most schools sexuality is muzzled and limited to an abstinence-only approach that became ensconced and even enshrined during eight years of the Bush administration, despite growing evidence that it was not effective either in preventing or diminishing STDs or teenage pregnancy.

Battles are being fought over what kinds of school groups can be formed, such as the student-initiated Gay-Straight Alliance, anti-harassment policies in public schools, and availability of age-appropriate reading material regarding lesbian and gay issues. The picture book *Heather Has Two Mommies* has been attacked and banned from many school districts.[16] Likewise, *And Tango Makes Three*, a beautifully illustrated book about two male penguins who co-parent an extra egg and are raising the female chick as their own, has made it to the top of the American Library Association's list of most banned books two years running. It usually makes the Top 10.[17]

As SCOTUS becomes even more conservative, many people rightly believe that the next attack will be to roll back LGBT rights, as has happened with women's rights. This has encouraged book burnings and local school boards prohibiting teachers from even using the word "gay" or discussing anything concerned with LGBT issues. Librarians are being told what can and cannot be purchased, with the list of banned books growing exponentially almost daily.

Another education issue relates to "magnet schools." As noted earlier, there has been a long-standing debate around deaf schools, oralist vs. signing and total communication, and mainstreaming deaf students into hearing classrooms. With LGBT students, it has been a bit more complex. In Manhattan, Harvey Milk School was a magnet school chartered in 2002 as a special haven for LGBT students. Ironically, it has been attacked by both conservatives and liberals, the former not wanting to give recognition or support to LGBT youth and the latter claiming that full inclusion and mainstreaming is the way to go.

Status of AIDS

This too is an immense subject, from the first identification of AIDS in 1981, when it was quickly and pejoratively labeled the "Gay Men's Disease," to now. The virus quickly morphed into something much broader and deeper. The next group of victims was IV drug users and those who received blood transfusions. Ryan White became the poster boy for the first "innocent" casualty of this disease. As a hemophiliac, he contracted AIDS through a blood transfusion of tainted blood. This led to his terribly unjust and misinformed expulsion from school, although evidence proved he posed no risk to other students. He died just over five years after his diagnosis, much longer than predicted.[18]

Although some few diehards, like Westboro Baptist Church pastor Fred Phelps mentioned above, still claim that AIDS is God's punishment for homosexuality, most people affected worldwide are now heterosexuals. The former administration got hung up on sexuality itself, not just homosexuality, and has refused to give money to nations promulgating birth control. Now AIDS is not the death sentence is no longer a death sentence and has even lost its "contagion" in virtually all cases. It has also lost its "contagion" stigma.

When we were away on a business trip a few years ago, Sheryl and I decided to drive by Fred Phelps's compound. On the other side of the street, a rainbow home had sprung up, a silent witness to a totally different worldview. Standing on the street between them felt like a continental divide of views representing diametrically different values. Girding up our courage, we stepped inside the rainbow house to introduce ourselves as clergywomen who were legally married to each other. All the occupants were young college students. I told them that they did not have to decide between being gay and belonging to a religious community. We build too many walls that need to be crossed or toppled.

As I pondered these deeply divisive worldviews, abhorring one and bringing love to the young inhabitants of the rainbow house across the street, Ezekiel 18:4 came to mind: "Behold, all souls are mine; as the soul of the father, so also the soul of the son is mine: the soul that sinneth, it shall die" (KJV). In the Bible, God uses this passage to convey that future generations will be held accountable for God's covenant terms with humanity. God knows that each new generation will likely betray the Lord but makes it clear that God will still hold them accountable. Phelps had thirteen children, fifty-four grandchildren, and a growing number of great-grandchildren. How were their lives impacted? How did his hateful and deeply harmful beliefs pass on to them and, by extension, their own children?

I cannot account for all of them, but I found proof that two of Phelps's children escaped the harmful dogma and cruel hatred of their father's church. The most widely known of the "escapees" is probably Megan Phelps-Roper, who wrote a stunning and powerful memoir, *Unfollow: A Memoir of Loving and Leaving the Westboro Baptist Church*.[19] She was indoctrinated daily by these hateful messages, but as she matured she reached out on the internet and found much that made her challenge her long-held beliefs about her father and his church. She found her future husband on the internet and also had a moral awakening, abandoning her tight-knit indoctrinated family for new forms of intimacy and community.

So far, more than twenty members of the Phelps family have left the church due to his behavior and WBC's practices. The second one who is well known is Nathan Phelps, who left the Kansas family house at eighteen, accusing his father of child abuse. While initially trying to find a new spiritual community of faith, ultimately he became an atheist and is sought after as a public speaker, where he has become an avid supporter of LGBT rights. He now resides in Canada. In 2021, Phelps was interviewed by the Freedom from Religion Foundation and told his riveting story of his father, relating the abuse he and his other twelve siblings endured. He shared about finally deciding to leave his father's church when he turned. The title of the documentary is *Nate Phelps: Former Westboro Baptist Church Member*.

On a personal note, my grown son David, now fifty-three, is a member of the Freedom from Religion Foundation. Another more well-known member is Ron Reagan, son of the conservative Republican president, Ronald Reagan. His liberal views contrast with those of his conservative father. He has been an outspoken critic of the modern-day Republican Party and claimed that his father would be "ashamed" over the influence of Donald Trump in the Republican Party.

It seems I am in good company with these two. While I am an active clergy member standing with the Christian Church (Disciples of Christ), we are an intentionally non-doctrinal church. I like to describe myself as a "heretical Christian." By that I mean I do not need to get into heated debates about the virgin birth, the divinity of Jesus, the resurrection, or even if there is a heaven or a hell. What motivates me every day is to follow the teachings of Jesus. That seems to be enough for me: actions, not words. Heaven or hell will have to wait!

As I reflected on this rigid and unbending hatred for gays still being taught in many churches, I found a phrase running through my mind, demanding my immediate attention. "You've got to be carefully taught" is a lyric from Rogers and Hammerstein's musical *South Pacific*, which debuted in 1949. One of the more well-known lines is "You've got to be taught to hate and fear…you've got to be carefully taught."

The captivating ditty sounds like something to share with small children, even as a singalong. But as I looked up more information about the song and its history, I found some interesting facts. In 1949, the United States was still recovering from the costly war fought on two fronts: against the Germans and the Japanese. The country was trying to recalibrate. So even a song as seemingly innocuous as this one stepped on many toes, almost stopping further production of the musical. *South Pacific* received scrutiny for its commentary regarding relationships between different races and ethnic groups. This seemingly innocuous song received widespread criticism. It was considered indecent, promoting interracial marriage and even the homosexual agenda. The creators risked their entire venture to make sure the song was included. Despite the ongoing and mounting attacks, Rogers and Hammerstein stood fast, and the song stayed in.

Racial prejudice was already ingrained in the country, but it was much worse against the Japanese, even Japanese Americans. While captured German POWs were allowed to do day labor at local farms, those of Japanese descent, even with US citizenship, were rounded up and their property impounded as they were herded to one of the eleven internment camps across America. They were spread out in California, Oregon, Arizona, Arkansas, Utah, and Colorado. These camps, also known as "relocation centers," were in remote areas surrounded by barbed wire and guard towers. Conditions in the camps were harsh, with families sharing barracks and living in tarpaper shacks. Inmates were often forced to work, with jobs ranging from doctors to teachers to laborers and mechanics.

In 2007, Sheryl and I visited this camp with a busload of other seminarians and professors. The camp housed over ten thousand evacuees of Japanese ancestry. It is in the middle of a desert between the High Sierras and Mt. Whitney, the highest peak in the US. When I asked Sheryl for her biggest "take" on the camp, the word that came to mind was "disturbing." For me it was seeing a now empty small pond the internees built to fill with fish. Others of them planted rows and rows of food to supplement their meager wartime rations. While many of the enlistees served in military intelligence both by translating Japanese documents and interrogating prisoners, most of them were in active service.

The 442nd Regimental Combat Team (RCT) was a highly decorated US Army unit composed of Japanese American soldiers during World War II, known for its courage and "Go for Broke" motto. The unit was formed in 1943 and was the most decorated unit in US military history for its size and length of service. The 442nd served in the European Theater of Operations, fighting in Italy, France, and Germany. These men fought bravely, courageously, to make sure America retained its freedoms, thought it continued being denied to their families. When the men who survived returned home, they found that in most cases their families' homes and businesses had been illegally confiscated by white neighbors. It would be a long road to rebuild what they had amassed, as loyal citizens, before the war.

My father was stationed at Pearl Harbor before and during World War II. He entered the Navy right after graduating from high school because he was the oldest of four children and the Depression hit his family hard. His monthly pay was able to keep them "afloat." He was a submariner, a torpedoman, who contracted diabetes while on long wartime activities away from base. The disease was precipitated by the high carb and sugar diet the men were subjected to for long periods between being able to resupply.

In retrospect, it was ironic to me that when I was a freshman in college a young Japanese classmate at Marymount College in Palos Verdes Estates, California, Tomoya Namura, often spent weekends at our home as a welcome and treasured guest. As I matured, it was even more ironic to me when my parents informed me I was not to date a Black boy. Since we lived de facto in a totally segregated town and I was enrolled in a Catholic girls' high school, I did not even either see or, God forbid, actually know a Black boy! My mother, when she met my spouse Sheryl, welcomed her with open arms. It reminds me that we all have "lists," possibly even unconscious, where we put groups of people into hierarchical orders of oppression.

During World War II, the community called Manzanar was hastily created in the high mountain desert country of California, east of the Sierras. Its purpose was to house thousands of Japanese American internees. One of the first families to arrive was the Wakatsukis, who were ordered to leave their fishing business in Long Beach and take with them only the belongings they could carry. For Jeanne Wakatsuki, a seven-year-old child, Manzanar became a way of life in which she struggled and adapted, observed and grew. For her father, it was essentially the end of his life. In *Farewell to Manzanar*, Jeanne Wakatsuki Houston recalls life at Manzanar through the eyes of the child she was.[20] She tells of her fear, confusion, and bewilderment as well as the dignity and great resourcefulness of people in oppressive and demeaning circumstances. Jeanne delivers a powerful first-person account that reveals her search for the meaning of Manzanar. *Farewell to Manzanar* has become a staple of curriculum in schools and on campuses across the country. The *San Francisco Chronicle* named it one of the twentieth century's 100 best nonfiction books from west of the Rockies.

My editor wondered how I got from the status of AIDS to Westboro Baptist to a Japanese internment camp. That is a good question. While my book focuses primarily on the "Wholly Other" statuses of two seemingly divergent groups, the Deaf and LGBT, primarily because I have personal experience with both, the purpose of this book is to remind the reader that these journeys are not unique but simply paradigmatic of how those who seem wholly other than us are more often than not treated as enemies. Thus, these perhaps seemingly random perambulations are to continue to shed light on other communities that have been marginalized as well.

Notes

[1] I found the NARTH mission statement via a Facebook post: https://www.facebook.com/GoodNeighborsWeVote/posts/narth-mission-statementwe-respect-the-right-of-all-individuals-to-choose-their-o/1603856707824861/.

[2] This statement appeared on the Exodus International home page, http://www.exodus-insternational.org/, accessed March 13, 2009. This website no longer exists since the group stopped operations in 2013.

[3] See "Exodus International," *Wikipedia*, https://en.wikipedia.org/wiki/Exodus_International.

[4] "The Homosexual Agenda," *Conservapedia*, https://www.conservapedia.com/Homosexual_Agenda, accessed April 24, 2025.

[5] Associated Press, "20 Years after Killing Matthew Shepard…," *Mercury News*, October 12, 2018, https://www.mercurynews.com/2018/10/12/matthew-shepard-killer-russell-henderson-interview-20-years/.

[6] *The Matthew Shepard Story*, written by John Wierick and Jacob Krueger, directed by Roger Spottiswoode, NBC, 88 minutes.

[7] Hudson Street Press, 2009.

[8] "Murder of James Byrd Jr.," *Wikipedia*, https://en.wikipedia.org/wiki/Murder_of_James_Byrd_Jr.

[9] "The Matthew Shepard and James Byrd, Jr., Hate Crimes Prevention Act of 2009," *Civil Rights Division (DOJ)*, https://www.justice.gov/crt/matthew-shepard-and-james-byrd-jr-hate-crimes-prevention-act-2009-0.

[10] "Becoming a People of Grace and Welcome to All," https://cdn.disciples.org/wp-content/uploads/2014/08/06162352/GA1327-BecomingAPeopleOfGraceAndWelcomeToAll-Final.pdf.

[11] "Hearing Accessibility for Participants," https://cdn.disciples.org/wp-content/uploads/2014/08/06162353/GA1322-HearingAccessibilityForParticipants-Final.pdf.

[12] See book description at https://www.amazon.com/Seven-Deadly-White-Christian-Nationalism/dp/1538167891.

[13] Harri Leigh, "Mennonite Church USA votes to affirm LGBTQ inclusion," *Fox43*, June 1, 2022, https://www.fox43.com/article/news/local/mennonite-policy-change-lgbtq-community/521-f0097809-7134-4016-a183-2931ee34e2a1.

[14] Edward Helmore, "10-year-old rape victim forced to travel…," *The Guardian*, July 3, 2022, https://www.theguardian.com/us-news/2022/jul/03/ohio-indiana-abortion-rape-victim.

[15] Ibid.

[16] *Heather Has Two Mommies*, written by Lesléa Newman and illustrated by Diane Souza (Alyson Books, 1989).

[17] *And Tango Makes Three*, written by Justin Peterson and Richard Parnell, illustrated by Henry Cole (Simon & Schuster Children's Publishing, 2005).

[18] For more, see "Ryan White," *Wikipedia*, https://en.wikipedia.org/wiki/Ryan_White.

[19] Megan Phelps-Roper, *Unfollow: A Memoir of Loving and Leaving the Westboro Baptist Church* (Farrar, Straus, and Giroux, 2019).

[20] Jeanne Wakatsuki Houston, *Farewell to Manzanar* (Boston: Houghton Mifflin, 1973).

Chapter 15
Some Major "Queer" Theological Ideas and Theologians

In this chapter, I detail how the word "queer" has changed in meaning over time. Now it stands for gay pride. For centuries before, it was considered something that was out of alignment, maybe even morally wrong. In my youth I was an unapologetically proud tomboy who competed and won against male age mates. They took to calling me a "bull dyke." I learned many years later that it was an insult, but even then, I wore it proudly because they were trying to insult me for being able to beat them at their own game.

Several decades after that, I was a clinic escort at an abortion services center in Portland, Oregon. We were trained in nonviolence and not allowed to speak up or shout back. One epithet that was thrown at me, between threats of death and imprisonment, was "Queen of the Dykes." I wish! What these anti-abortion protesters viewed as the highest insult I wore as a mark of pride. Then, in 1992, after our long walk of protest from Eugene to Portland, Oregon, our group, "The Walk Against Hate: The Walk for Love and Justice," was accorded the high honor of being first in the procession, right behind the Dykes on Bikes. The river flows on, times change, and sometimes, if we live long enough, people change too!

The Changing Meaning of "Queer"

The meaning of "queer" is a study in both fluidity and confusion. The word is

An umbrella term used to describe gender/sexual/romantic orientations or identities that fall outside of societal norms. Historically, queer has been used as an epithet/slur against the LGBTQ+ community. Some people have reclaimed the word queer and self identify in opposition to assimilation. For some, this reclamation is a celebration of not fitting into social norms. Not all people who identify as LGBTQIA use "queer" to describe themselves. For example, those of earlier generations are typically averse to self-identifying as queer. The term is often considered hateful when used by those who do not identify as LGBTQIA.[1]

Another "queer" term was used in one of our favorite TV shows, *The Murdoch Mysteries*.[2] It takes place in Toronto, Canada, in the early twentieth century. Canada was granted the right of self-governance in 1867 but did not gain full autonomy until 1931. In one plot, the police become aware of a woman's scheme for a boy to pretend to be hit by a car, then have the driver offer to pay to take the child to the hospital. This is an example of what came to be known as "queer plunging." The term originated with people who threw themselves in the water in order to be saved by their accomplices, who carried them to one of the houses appointed by the Humane Society for the recovery of drowned persons. There, the society awarded them a guinea each, and the supposed drowned persons, pretending they were driven to that extreme action by great necessity, were frequently sent away with a contribution in their pockets. This definition is taken from *The 1811 Dictionary of the Vulgar Tongue*, originally by Francis Grose.[3] By the 1980s, the label "queer" began to be reclaimed from its questionable or pejorative use as a neutral or positive self-identifier by LGBT people.

Emerging and Clarifying of the Term "Homosexuality"

It was only in 1869 that homosexuality was clearly defined. This classification was first used by Karl-Maria Kertbeny and then published in two pamphlets in 1869. It became the standard term when used by Richard von Krafft-Ebing in his *Psychopathia Sexualis: The Classic Study of Deviant Sex*.[4] Preceding Freud's *Three Contributions to the Theory of Sex*[5] by more than twenty years, Krafft-Ebing's *Psychopathia Sexualis* pioneered the psychological study of sexual behavior. This classic nineteenth-century work on sexual aberration addressed such previously taboo subjects as bestiality, cunnilingus and fellatio, fetishism, incest, masochism, masturbation, nymphomania, and sadism, making it the first serious attempt to catalog and define such "deviations."

For almost one hundred years, *Psychopathia Sexualis* stood as the world's most informative volume about sexual deviation. Arguably the most important precursor to Freud in the study of human sexuality, Krafft-Ebing introduced ideas and concepts that greatly influenced the works of Alfred Kinsey and Masters and Johnson. In his own time, Krafft-Ebing was both praised and damned for this volume. Some psychiatrists denounced the work as an immoral apology for perversion and deviance, while others recognized the immense service the author had done for an unjustly neglected area of study. Although sometimes dated by the beliefs and state of knowledge of the time it was written, *Psychopathia Sexualis* is essential (and immensely entertaining) as one of the most important documents in humankind's modern effort to understand itself.

The Word "Queer" in Today's Lexicon

As language shifts, terms take on new meanings. But when is it appropriate for media organizations to reflect those changes?

In recent years, the word "queer" has been increasingly seen and heard in NPR reporting, upsetting some listeners. One listener from Illinois wrote, "I am a gay man, and I did not spend my entire life being called queer as a slur for journalists to accept it as reclaimed. It isn't." Another listener wrote to us from Massachusetts: "If you have made a decision to allow LGBT people to be referred to as 'queers' on the air, then please say so and justify that decision ON THE AIR."

After a report from *Weekend Edition Saturday* on the LGBTQ dating app Grindr used the word "queer" multiple times, one listener from Kentucky wrote: "…it deeply disturbs me that national media may be getting on the 'labeling me as a queer' train."[6]

This reminds me of a workshop I did with a gay man in Ashland, Oregon, in the late 1980s. I was then working part-time at the Quaker social justice organization American Friends Service Committee in Portland. The head of the queer rights office and I were doing the presentation when a middle-aged white woman raised her hand and said that she appreciated our reappropriation of the word "gay." Evidently her father had used that word for her when she was a young child, and she wanted to reappropriate it. I cannot remember how we responded to her, but it does serve as an example that a living language cannot be static, nor should it be.

A story in the *Des Moines Register* also addressed the topic after it published a story that used "queer" in quoting a person speaking about themselves and their community, "prompting readers to ask why any newspaper would print such an offensive and insensitive term." The *Register* responded that it refers to GLAAD for guidance on its use of the word.[7] Jason DeRose, previously Western Bureau Chief and senior editor overseeing NPR's LGBTQ reporting and now their Religion Correspondent, said that when NPR does use the word "queer," it is not done as an afterthought but is the result of much conversation by newsroom leaders. A longtime member of the Association of LGBTQ+ Journalists (NLGJA), DeRose noted that the discussion is also not new for people within the LGBTQ community. And after over eleven years at NPR, he has witnessed a wider shift to accept the word. "What you can see is an evolution, and I think you see that in the culture at large," said DeRose. "There was a time when people said 'homosexual.'" DeRose went on to say that "homosexual" is no longer advised for use in journalism.[8]

Queer representation in mainstream media is owed to hard-won campaigns for public acceptance. There are affirmative examples like the show *Heartstopper*,[9] which gives queer people the wholesome, happy endings they were so long denied, and *Queer Eye*,[10] which highlights the skills of five gay professionals who help others change their lives. Perhaps the words will continue to ebb and flow, but the goal should always be to respect the community and try to use the terms they prefer.

Introduction to "Queer" Theology

"Queer" theology is a large and growing body. To a much lesser degree, there is beginning to be a "deaf" theology, not simply about provided visibility and services to the deaf but a theology coming from the depths of life experiences of the deaf. There is initially a big distinction, however, when considering queer theology versus deaf theology. On the one hand, although LGBT people are sometimes marginalized, excluded, and even demonized, it is because of what some perceive as a "moral" failure rather than a physical one. This is an important consideration at first.

The three ways the two groups will be linked later in the book is that (1) both of them challenge an overly simplistic and inaccurate binary system for labeling people (e.g., "heterosexual" or "homosexual," "hearing" or "deaf"); (2) both are "embodied," challenging our beliefs about the role and sacredness of the body; (3) and, in my opinion, there is a call for a particular kind of Christology based on a man who some say is a God-man and is too human, too wounded, too just like us!

Challenging the Binary System of Colonialism

Be it sexism, heterosexism, racism, ableism, or numerous other forms the colonial binary system is based on several faulty assumptions: (1) the "Other" can easily be identified and overpowered or assimilated; (2) the "Other" is part of a binary system with no confusion or blurring of the lines; (3) the "Other" has nothing to offer us that can be of use to us or enrich us. When one chips away at the seemingly indestructible binary system of "us vs. them," then the abilities to identify, isolate, and shut the Other off from the possibility of value or giftedness are eroded as well.

In light of this deeply held yet inherently flawed concept of rigid dualism comes a procession of "queers"—bisexuals, transgendered, "lipstick lesbians," the Gay Olympics, Log Cabin Republicans—who definitively prove that sexuality can neither be clearly defined nor fixed firmly in homeostasis. If there isn't a clear-cut definition, diagnosis, and separation of heterosexual vs. homosexual, what kind of a theology might this be?

In *The Sexual Theologian: Essays on Sex, God and Politics*, the authors claim that "Queer theology strives instead for differentiation and plurality. Queer theology is in this sense equivalent to a call for biodiversity in theology" and "resistance against heterosexual knowing." They write, "queer theory has deregulated the binary myths of the subjects of theology, and in doing that it has deregulated our representations of God."[11] One need only peruse Roughgarden's Evolution's Rainbow:

Diversity, Gender and Sexuality in Nature and People to get a crash course in biology's rich and uniquely creative diversity—across species and time.[12] As a transgendered woman, Roughgarden, a professor of biological sciences at Stanford University, brings her personal experience into the fray as she investigates the extraordinarily diverse and unique contributions that species, from seahorses to humans, from invertebrates to mammals, bring to the process of maintaining the species.

The nineteenth century saw the development of the Linnaean system of classification of species based on a binary system, coupled with the development of the periodic table of elements, that sought to investigate, explore, then "fix" nature into a closed-system pattern. The system was challenged, time and time again, by the sheer explosion of biology out of its lifeless boxes. Roughgarden concludes that rainbows subvert the human goal of classifying nature and that the most basic question faced by evolutionary biology is whether variation within a species is good in its own right or simply a collection of impurities every species is stuck with. She also says that even evolutionary biologists are divided on this issue.

Embodiment

There is no way to speak of the LGBT community without addressing embodiment. Before Stonewall, one was likely to see only a heterosexist projection of sexuality, with the man determining the how, where, and what of sexual expression with his wife and also fueling the pornographic underground of prostitutes, "playmates," etc. Until 1976, marital rape was legal, codifying and encouraging male sexual violence against their mates. It was based on power, privilege, and misogyny. Then along came the "queers," overturning male dominance, seeing sexual expression as something to be celebrated and enjoyed, reclaiming the pleasures of the body without the opposition of a negative, anti-body, and anti-sexual theological inheritance. (This is not to claim that people who identify as queer are unaffected by anti-body and anti-sex messages. If only this were the case!) Embodiment is a major aspect of queer theology, so this section is simply a "sampler" of some of the leading players rather than a systematic overview.

Marcella Althaus-Reid, in her previously mentioned book The Sexual Theologian, further claims that norms are easy conveniences for those who like surveys and statistics but not for those who live in the world. She says that life can never be normal for those who embrace the flesh as divine, those who are lovers of God through that flesh in all its diverse glory. She concludes that any theology that has incarnation at its heart is queer indeed.

Carter Heyward, an Episcopalian priest, takes the idea of "flesh in all its diverse glory" explicitly into the realm of the erotic:

> [A]s we come to experience the erotic as sacred, we begin to know ourselves as holy and to imagine ourselves sharing in the creation of one another and of our common well-being.... [T]he erotic blesses us with transcendence and immanence. She enables us to cross boundaries and draws us more fully into ourselves. She compels us to touch one another without fear and allows us to go into ourselves to feel safe. Teaching us a rhythm of transcendence and immanence, of reaching out and going in, of letting go and holding on, she enables us to make love/justice. She teaches us to be friends.[13]

Following closely on the publication of Carter's book was a statement from the Presbyterians in 1991 on human sexuality. This report

> ...judiciously examines the legacy of human injustice perpetuated by Christianity's adoption of a Platonic dualism that counterposes the body and soul, and hence sexuality with spirituality. This report clarifies that dualistic paradigms inevitably generate other antagonistic dualisms that subsequently produce injustices such as sexism and heterosexism.
>
> It correctly suggests that if the church is to promote gender and sexual justice, it must rethink its theology of the body/sexuality, abandon its allegiance to dualistic paradigms, and construct a new sexual ethic. This new ethic will promote "justice-love," where the "gift of sexuality and God's gracious call to be in loving, caring, mutual relations with [all] others" is nurtured and celebrated.[14]

There are numerous other theologians whose contributions are critical to incarnational theology, such as James Nelson and Joan Timmerman. Nelson's book, *Embodiment: An Approach to Sexuality and Christian Theology*, was groundbreaking. His last chapter, "The Church as Sexual Community," must have raised—or even singed—a few eyebrows![15] In his next book on the subject, *Between Two Gardens: Reflections on Sexuality and Religious Experience*, he states, "While human sexuality is not the whole of our personhood, it is a basic dimension of that personhood. While it does not determine all thought, feeling and action, it does permeate and affect all of these."[16]

Joan Timmerman followed soon after with her book, *The Mardi Gras Syndrome: Rethinking Christian Sexuality*. She gave it this title because in the Middle Ages Christians were required to limit sex to Tuesdays. Her main thesis is that "[h]uman sexuality participates in the sacred; it is capable of revealing God and God's action in human life, and of transforming human existence from an isolated and disconnected experience to one of unity and ecstasy."[17]

Breaking out of the body-soul dichotomy box is hard for those weaned and fed on Platonic ideals and anti-body theologies deeply imbedded in Christian tradition from the time of Augustine. It is difficult to think about our own bodies, our own sexuality, our own spirituality as somehow intertwined rather than at war. What happens when we have this discourse around the life, the body, the incarnation, and the mission of Jesus? The stakes rise tremendously.

Christological Considerations

How we view Jesus is crucial to how we understand our own embodiment and even our own sexuality. Our theologies of Jesus run the full spectrum from Docetism to full embodiment. The Docetists stemmed from the late first century CE, taking their name from the Greek word *dokein*, meaning "to seem." A branch of Gnosticism, which believed in a split between the unseen world of perfection and the imperfect world of the flesh, Docetists applied this belief to explain away the humanness and suffering of Jesus, claiming that it just "seemed" as if he suffered. They took it even further, stating that Jesus only seemed to have a body. While Docetism was soon declared heretical, it continued in a subversive form, infecting incarnational theology for centuries.

In the section on deaf theology, I will treat in more detail the theology of a disabled God, but here I want to explore the implications and ramifications of a sexual God. Carter Heyward summarizes the "problem": "As Mary Daly notes, Christianity has become, over its two millennia, a necrophilial religion centered around a dead man. Because the church has established itself as a custodian of misogynist, erotophobic theological values, the body of Christ is losing its appeal for many faithful churchwomen."[18] Marcella Althaus-Reid builds on this idea, claiming that "[w]hen we think about Christ, we do not think about a man, we think about a God/man, a celibate batman, batteries included to supply his head with that halo of light which we frequently see in paintings."[19]

One way to look at this "neutering" or "desexing" of Jesus is through great works of art. In *The Sexuality of Christ in Renaissance Art and in Modern Oblivion*, Leo Steinberg examines portrayals of both the infant Christ and the suffering and dying Christ in regard to their depiction of his genitalia. I was planning on skimming it, but the prose as well as the art drew me in. The book begins with the author's main thesis:

> The first necessity is to admit a long-suppressed matter of fact: that Renaissance art, both north and south of the Alps, produced a large body of devotional imagery in which the genitalia of the Christ Child, or of the dead Christ, receive such demonstrative emphasis that one must recognize an *ostentatio genitalium* comparable to the canonic *ostentatio vulnerum*,

the showing forth of the wounds. In many hundreds of pious, religious works, from before 1400 to past the mid-15th century, the ostensive unveiling of the Child's sex, or the touching, protecting or presentation of it, is the main action. And the emphasis recurs in images of the dead Christ, or of the mystical Man of Sorrows. All of which has been tactfully overlooked for half a millennium.[20]

Steinberg's book features a nude study and an edited sculpture of *The Risen Christ*. The statue was also nude, but even now the original statue in Santa Maria sopra Minerva stands, as Steinberg writes,

> ...disfigured by a brazen breechclout. But the intended nudity of Michelangelo's figure was neither a licentious conceit nor thoughtless truckling to antique example. If Michelangelo denuded his Risen Christ, he must have seen that a loincloth would convict these genitalia of being "pudenda," thereby denying the very work of redemption which promised to free human nature from its Adamic contagion of shame.[21]

For Steinberg, the eternal, by definition, experiences neither death nor generation:

> If the godhead incarnates itself to suffer a human fate, it takes on the condition of being both death-bound and sexed. The mortality it assumes is correlative with sexuality, since it is by procreation that the race, though consigned to death individually, endures collectively to fulfill the redemptive plan. Therefore, to profess that God once embodied himself in a human nature is to confess that the eternal, there and then, became mortal and sexual. Thus understood, the evidence of Christ's sexual member serves as the pledge of God's humanation.[22]

In *Queering Christ: Beyond Jesus Acted Up*, Robert Goss continues to comment on the significance of Christ's "sexual member":

> In the great cathedrals hung paintings of the Holy Family in which Mary herself deliberately spreads the infant's thighs so that the pious might gaze at his genitals in wonder. In other paintings the Magi are depicted gazing intently at Jesus' uncovered loins as if expecting revelation. In still others Jesus' genitals are being touched and fondled by his mother, by St. Anne, and by himself. So also, in the paintings of the passion and crucifixion, the adult Jesus is depicted as thoroughly sexual. In some, his hand cups his genitals in death, in others the loincloth of the suffering Christ is protruding with an unmistakable erection.[23]

There have been many attempts to explain away this overwhelming preponderance of evidence, to "erase" even a hint of sexuality. James Nelson powerfully names not only the depth of our discomfort with a sexual Savior but also what happens to us when we cannot—or will not—look at what a naked, exposed, sexually potent Savior might do for our theology:

> That Jesus should be a laughing, crying, sweating, urinating, defecating, orgasmic, sensuous bundle of flesh just as we are seems incomprehensible. Then the reverse is also true. Because we find it difficult to believe that God genuinely embraced total flesh in Jesus, we have trouble believing that incarnation can and does occur in us too. Lacking the conviction that God not only blesses human flesh from afar but also intimately embraces and permeates the body-selves which we are, expressing divine presence and activity in the world through us, we find it difficult to incorporate our sexuality into our spirituality.[24]

Althaus-Reid takes this idea even further by linking it to the Eucharist and the orthodox understanding of transubstantiation: "In the Eucharist, according to the dogma of transubstantiation, 'God is what you eat, that fetish of bread and wine. God is what you digest, perspire and excrete from your body. God is the transit of bread and wine in your stomach and bowels.'"[25]

A closing point made in *Indecent Theology* warrants in-depth discussion beyond the scope of this paper: a challenge to the inexorable "maleness" of Christ. Althaus-Reid states, "Jesus has been represented in art as nude, half nude, or dressed according to the fashion of Palestine at his time, but this is not all the dressing to which we are referring here. He has been dressed theologically as a heterosexually orientated (celibate) man. Jesus with erased genitalia; Jesus minus erotic body."[26] She illustrates this by speaking of the still-controversial bronze sculpture of *Christa* by Edwina Sandys: "The Christa is another example of obscenity. It undresses the masculinity of God and produces feelings and questionings which were suppressed by centuries of identificatory masculine processes with God. Why, for instance, is the tortured male body of Christ less offensive and infinitely more divine than a woman's tortured body?"[27]

TIME magazine featured a lead article following *Christa*'s exhibition at St. John the Divine in Manhattan at a Maundy Thursday service in 1984.

> The Maundy Thursday services at the Episcopal Cathedral of St. John the Divine in Manhattan included such now familiar symbols of a progressive liturgy as a dramatic reading and a symbolic dance. But when a four-foot bronze statue of Jesus on the cross was unveiled, gasps could be heard

throughout the main chapel. The Christus was, in fact, a Christa, complete with undraped breasts and rounded hips.

The work, created in 1975 by Sculptor Edwina Sandys, 45, for the United Nations' Decade for Women, had been shown in galleries and art exhibits, but it had never before been displayed in a church. To New York Suffragan Bishop Walter Dennis, it was a "desecration" of Christian symbols. He urged parishioners to write the diocese's presiding bishop, the Rt. Rev. Paul Moore Jr., "if it shocks you as much as it did me." Cathedral Dean James Parks Morton, who organized the display with Moore's concurrence, responded that the effort to "send a positive message to women" had upset only the same people who oppose ordination for women. Said Sandys (who is the granddaughter of Winston Churchill): "It shows that the church still has power, and that people do care."

As for those who made a point of walking behind the cathedral's main altar to have a look during the statue's ten-day showing, the reactions were mixed, but rarely mild. It was "not at all blasphemous" to Katherine Austin, who thought it reflected a mystic Christian view that "sees Christ as our mother." Beverly Stewart, on the other hand, said, "It's disgraceful. God and Christ are male. They're playing with a symbol we've believed in for all our lives." The Christa seemed to be doing her job as a focus for provocation, if not of prayer.[28]

Heyward also reflects on the insights contemplating this controversial sculpture can give us:

> Christa is a controversial concept. She represents an embodied energy that, if released among us, will change the world. Among progressive Christians, there is nothing especially alarming about the religious mandate to change the world, a goal easily affirmed because it seems safely remote from our daily lives. In the context of sexist, erotophobic patriarchy, Christa, unlike the male Christ, is controversial because her body signals a crying need for woman-affirming (nonsexist), erotic (nonerotophobic) power that, insofar as we share it, will transform a world that includes our own most personal lives in relation.[29]

I had the pleasure of seeing this powerful statue firsthand when it was exhibited at the Bade Institute at the Pacific School of Religion. I can't remember the particular date, but I still remember standing there with a combination of shock and awe. In front of me were several clergymen in clerical collars making derogatory comments about the figure. I don't remember the details of their conversation, but they served as a living reminder of how the patriarchy had shut out all women, and me in particular, from the fullness of revelation, always having to be filtered through and interpreted by men.

As we review the major literature of Queer Christology, we can see that it eschews a high Christology that places Jesus, incarnate (well, sort of!) God-man, temporarily in the world of messy human experience and at times all-too-messy physical reality in favor of one that values, delights in, and exalts the holiness of being embodied, not just for us but for Jesus as well.

Conclusion

I have examined "queer" theology through three lenses: (1) the myth of the binary system; (2) the embodiedness of "queer" theory and praxis; (3) and an approach to Christology that ironically but inevitably "lowers" the status of a sexless, necrophilic, static God-man to that of a living, breathing, laughing, crying, suffering, rejoicing human—like one of us. And that makes all the difference.

As I finished this chapter, the name "Joan Roughgarden" came to mind as a memory emerged from my time at Pacific School of Religion (2006–2009). A Stanford biologist, she had just finished her book *Evolution's Rainbow: Diversity, Gender and Sexuality in Nature and People*. She had come to the campus to do a presentation of the new book. Afterwards, we all went out to the lawn together and circled around, holding hands. I stood right next to her.

That in itself would not be such a big deal, except that she was born male and had transitioned to female. This was twenty years ago, and the word "transgender" and people who actually were transgender had just begun to attract the attention of the larger community. Yet as we stood in that circle, hand touching hand as a community of faith, her hand felt just like any other hand I had held or might hold in the future—a warm, vibrant, loving connection between not only our spirits and minds but also our bodies. Another veil or separation had parted, and we truly became "Holy Other" to each other in that moment.

Notes

[1] "LGBTQIA Resource Center Glossary: Queer," *LGBTQIA Resource Center UC Davis*, https://lgbtqia.ucdavis.edu/educated/glossary#q.

[2] Based on *Detective Murdoch* series by Maureen Jennings, developed by R. B. Carney, Cal Coons, and Alexandra Zarowny, Citytv and CBC, 2008–present.

[3] Francis Grose, *1811 Dictionary of the Vulgar Tongue: A Dictionary of Buckish Slang, University Wit, and Pickpocket Eloquence* (republished by Cavalier Classics, 2015).

[4] Richard von Krafft-Ebing, *Psychopathia Sexualis: The Classic Study of Deviant Sex* (Stuttgart: Verlag Von Ferdinand Enke, 1886).

[5] Sigmund Freud, *Three Contributions to the Theory of Sexuality* (Leipzig and Vienna: Deuticke, 1905).

[6] Juliette Rocheleau, "A Former Slur Is Reclaimed, and Listeners Have Mixed Feelings," *NPR*, August 21, 2019, https://www.npr.org/sections/publiceditor/2019/08/21/752330316/a-former-slur-is-reclaimed-and-listeners-have-mixed-feelings.

[7] Quoted in Commentary, "From LGBTQ to Queer," *The Paper*, June 1, 2021, https://abq.news/2021/06/from-lgbtq-to-queer/.

[8] Rocheleau, "A Former Slur Is Reclaimed."

[9] Written by Alice Oseman, based on her graphic novel series, directed by Euros Lyn and Andy Newbery, See-Saw Films, 2022–present.

[10] Created by David Collins (reboot), Scout Productions and ITV Entertainment, 2018–present.

[11] Marcella Althaus-Reid and Lisa Isherwood, *The Sexual Theologian: Essays on Sex, God and Politics* (Bloomsbury Publishing, 2005).

[12] Joan Roughgarden, *Evolution's Rainbow: Diversity, Gender and Sexuality in Nature and People* (University of California Press, 2005).

[13] Carter Heyward, *Touching our Strength: The Erotic as Power and the Love of God* (San Francisco: HarperCollins Publishing, 1989), 114.

[14] *Presbyterians and Human Sexuality: 1991* (Louisville, KY: Office of the General Assembly Presbyterian Church (U.S.A.), https://www.pcusa.org/sites/default/files/human-sexuality1991.pdf. Also see Marvin Ellison and Sylvia Horson-Smith, eds., *Body and Soul: Rethinking Sexuality as Justice-Love* (Cleveland: The Pilgrim Press, 2003), 100.

[15] James B. Nelson, *Embodiment: An Approach to Sexuality and Christian Theology* (Minneapolis: Augsburg Press, 1979).

[16] James B. Nelson, *Between Two Gardens: Reflections on Sexuality and Religious Experience* (New York: The Pilgrim Press, 1983).

[17] Joan Timmerman, *The Mardi Gras Syndrome: Rethinking Christian Sexuality* (New York: Crossroad, 1985).

[18] Carter Heyward, *Touching Our Strength: The Erotic as Power and the Love of God* (San Francisco: HarperCollins Publishing, 1989).

[19] Marcella Althaus-Reid, *Indecent Theology: Theological Perversions in Sex, Gender and Politics* (London and New York: Routledge, 2000), 114.

[20] Leo Steinberg, *The Sexuality of Christ in Renaissance Art and in Modern Oblivion* (Chicago: The University of Chicago Press, 1983), 3.

[21] Ibid., 21.

[22] Ibid.

[23] Robert E. Goss, *Queering Christ: Beyond Jesus Acted Up* (Cleveland: The Pilgrim Press, 2002), 149.

[24] Nelson, *Between Two Gardens*, 17.

[25] Althaus-Reid, *Indecent Theology*, 92.

[26] Ibid., 114.

[27] Ibid., 111

[28] "Religion: Vexing Christa," *TIME*, May 7, 1984, https://time.com/archive/6699995/religion-vexing-christa/.

[29] Heyward, *Touching Our Strength*.

Chapter 16
Theologies of Disability

"By His wounds we are healed." (1 Peter 2:24, NIV)

The first theologian mentioned below, Nancy Eisland, makes a good point about churches trying to accommodate people with disabilities. Yes, but not all people with disabilities are visible to the naked eye or exposed ear. I have one of the least known and mostly forgotten or ignored disabilities: hearing loss. While it is obvious whether or not a building has physical access, often places like churches fail to recognize the need to reach out to people with hearing loss, virtually all of whom need some sort of assistive listening technology such as a hearing loop. A well-installed hearing loop is invisible, and most people with hearing loss—20 percent of the population and increasing to 50 percent as we age—will not speak up about it but suffer silently in their pews until they feel that church is no longer worth attending. To become visible, we must be heard!

One of my now-funny encounters happened years ago when I saw a sign posted on a McDonald's: "We have hearing assistance." Not believing my eyes, I drove up to the order window, asked what kind of hearing assistance they had, and the server did not have a clue. I asked to speak with a manager, who would be at the next window. When I drove up, he had no idea what I was talking about. He did, however, state that they had a menu in braille. Then he told me that he was majoring in deaf studies at a local university. As I drove off, I was tempted to drive around for a while with my eyes shut, then return to the fast-food joint and ask them to give me the braille menu!

This issue comes up frequently at motels. One had a sign claiming they offered hearing assistance. I asked the clerk what was available, and she said she did not know what that meant and went off to ask her supervisor. She came back with the (in)famous words, "We have ear plugs for people who are wanting to shut out the noise."

That's hearing loss in a nutshell. We are not only the largest group labeled "disabled" but the one most misunderstood!

Introduction

Before launching into a theology specific to deafness, I will first explore the theologies of disability. I begin with Nancy Eiesland's *The Disabled God: Toward a Liberatory Theology of Disability*.[1] The book has become a classic and a touchstone for those doing work with various groups. But first, a note of warning: as already mentioned previously, by and large, deaf people do not do well wearing the "disabled" mantle, preferring to think of themselves as a linguistic and cultural minority.

Nancy Eisland

One of the most noteworthy theologians of disability is Nancy Eiesland. Considering herself disabled, she bluntly reflects on the church's role in the continued "disabling" of the disabled:

> Rather than being a structure of empowerment, the church has more often supported the societal structures and attitudes that have treated people with disabilities as objects of pity and paternalism.... Today most denominations and many local congregations realize that church facilities should be constructed or altered to encourage the presence of persons with disabilities. Yet little effort has been made to promote the full participation of people with disabilities in the life of the church.[2]

Eiesland argues that there is a tendency to try to both rationalize and homogenize human experience and arrive at something approximating social consensus. But, referring to the work of Rebecca Chopp, Eiesland states unequivocally that theology needs to embrace difference, specificity, embodiment, and ultimately transformation.

In spite of this, many have been left out. It is especially apparent when observing the way those with disabilities have been treated by the church: "I concentrate on the 'mixed blessing' of the body in the real, lived experience of people with disabilities and explicitly deconstruct any norms which are part of the unexpressed agenda of 'normal embodiment.'"[3] Disabled people have probably been marginalized more than any other group. Part of that marginalization is through their naming as "disabled," a term many of them, particularly although not exclusively the deaf, abhor. Eiesland points out, "[A]s linguists and anthropologists know, the act of naming someone or something grants the namer power over the named. Historically, rather than naming ourselves, the disabled have been named by medical and scientific professionals or by people who denied our full personhood."[4]

For Eiesland, accessibility is not simply modifications that allow fuller access to shared public space. It must also, and perhaps more importantly, be understood as participation throughout society as a legally protected right. She claims, however, that society tends to put the onus on the disabled person, whose needs seem unique and at times extraordinary, rather than addressing society-wide issues of inclusion and exclusion. She sees accessibility as making available "the same choices accorded to able-bodied people. It also means opening the meaning of 'normal' to the ordinary lives of people with disabilities."[5]

This does not mean erasing or pretending to erase very real differences and unique experiences that the disabled bring to the process of living. Being or becoming "normal" cannot mean just that the disabled have their particular disability minimized but that the disabilities themselves may "disclose new categories and models of thinking and being."[6] This insight of a different yet powerful way of "knowing" will become apparent when deaf theology is explored further on.

For Eiesland, the *ikon* of God that most fits her thesis of full inclusion while recognizing and respecting differences is the resurrected Jesus Christ. For the frightened male disciples, huddled in an upstairs room, Jesus Christ appears transformed but still with the wounds that marked his painful and bloody crucifixion. Only one disciple, Thomas, has the courage to reach out and touch them, to understand not only with his mind but also with his heart and hands that all human experiences can be claimed, redeemed, and transformed. Who else will dare to reach out and touch those who often frighten us, confuse us, perhaps even repulse us? For it is only in the touching that we experience the gifts they bring us.

Other Perspectives on the Disabled God

Burton Cooper was one of the earliest writers to propose the concept of a "disabled" God. He does, however, focus on suffering, which deaf people in particular reject as not describing their condition.[7]

Regarding the "disabled Christ," Amanda Shao Tan, professor of theology at the Asian Theological Seminary in Manila, defines "disabled" as a functional limitation that can easily be applied to Christ.[8]

R. McCloughry and W. Morris state, "Christ has taken his experience up into God. This Christ ascends into his glory but even in his glory he bears the marks as well as the experience of his physical body." In heaven, they argue, "Christ is not 'normalized' to be like 'perfect' human beings, but…the wounds and marks of earth are somehow transformed in heaven."[9]

John Hull reflects on the experience of God through physical blindness in his book, *In the Beginning There Was Darkness: A Blind Person's Conversations with the Bible*.[10]

Mary Weir was the first person to suggest in a publication that God is deaf. She shows how this is distinctively an experience linked to the incarnation: the Logos is concrete and tangible.[11] Thus, she departs from a major strand of disability theology in seeing deafness as focused on a strength, not as a perceived lack that must be compensated for.

Conclusion: A Christology for All

There is much to ponder in this section and many paths for fleshing out a theology, specifically a Christology that is not based on a perfect, otherworldly, resurrected Christ who sits comfortably at the right hand of the Father, having not only recovered from his chancy and short time on earth as incarnate, subject to all of the failings—and triumphs—of human flesh. What kind of a Christology would we have if we fully embraced the physicality of Jesus, including the wounds so apparent in his crucifixion, not as erasable but as embraceable? That, I would argue, is the kind of incarnation that speaks not only to those labeled "disabled," such as those who are deaf, but to all of us, for we all have wounds, either seen or unseen, and it is through them, not around or above them, that we can find our place in the Son.

Notes

[1] Nancy L. Eiesland, *The Disabled God: Toward a Liberatory Theology of Disability* (Nashville: Abingdon Press, 1994).

[2] Ibid., 20.

[3] Ibid.

[4] Ibid. 25.

[5] Ibid., 28.

[6] Ibid., 31.

[7] Burton Cooper, "The Disabled God," *Theology Today* 49, no. 2 (1992): 173–182.

[8] Amanda Shao Tan, "The Disabled Christ," *Transformation* 15, no. 4 (1998): 8-14.

[9] R. McCloughry and W. Morris, *Making a World of Difference: Christian Reflections on Disability* (London: SPCK, 2002), 146.

[10] John M. Hull, *In the Beginning There Was Darkness: A Blind Person's Conversation with the Bible* (London: SCM Press, 2001).

[11] Mary Kathryn Weir, "Made Deaf in God's Image," in International Ecumenical Working Group, *The Place of Deaf People in the Church* (Northampton: Visible Communications, 1996), 1–10. Cited in Wayne Morris, *Theology without Words: Theology in the Deaf Community* (Hampshire, England: Ashgate, 2008), 147.

Chapter 17
Beginning Considerations in Theologies of the Deaf

Before my own sudden-onset deafness, I never had cause to ponder the intricacies of being deaf. Although I had gradually lost hearing in one ear due to a benign tumor, which only took out my hearing and years later made the right side of my face sag but did not threaten my life, I compensated. I put people on the side of the good ear, tried to train my spouse to speak clearly while not walking away with her back turned, and looked twice both ways before crossing the street (I was no longer able to figure out the direction of a sound). Overall, it was just a mild inconvenience that did not in any real or deep way affect how I lived my life. When, as a minister, I *did* think about issues of hearing loss, I assumed, incorrectly as later experience would teach me, that if a church had a sign language interpreter for the deaf, that would cover *all* contingencies.

I was proved very wrong when I was tossed precipitously into a silent world! For seven months, my only communication with hearing people was through *my* speaking but *their* writing. I no longer went to church, where I would be de facto segregated. The most frequently asked question from hearing people was, "Do you lip-read?" Unfortunately, waking up deaf did not come with the compensation of suddenly being able to lip-read or understand sign.

Over the next few months, as I figured out the landscape of my new world, its unchartered territory, its pitfalls and traps, and, strangely, its blessings as well, I discovered that there is no simple, easy, "clean" distinction that separates the hearing and deaf worlds. There are the hard-of-hearing, with varying degrees of hearing loss, much of it happening over a long time. And then there is the smallest group, the late-deafened. There was really no "one size fits all" category of deafness, as contrasted to and opposed to hearing.

There are the born and culturally deaf, for whom ASL is either their primary or only language. Even in this category, it is not so simple. Some born deaf, due to the influence of the medical model and the stress on oralism as the *only* way to communicate, still try to function—with varying degrees of success—in the hearing world by lipreading and trying to articulate words they have never been able to hear. Others eschew anything to do with oralism, relying on signs alone to communicate both with other deaf people and, through interpreters, with the hearing world.

This chapter is not about those who are hard-of-hearing or late-deafened, although their numbers are large and growing (more than 37,000,000 adults in the United States have some form of hearing loss that impacts their lives in major ways). I want to focus here on those who are part of the Deaf community, who were either born deaf or became deaf prelingually (before acquired speech).

Embodied—A New Language

The Deaf community has a sense of embodiment that is similar to that of the LGBT community. While it is not explicitly projected by the heterosexist community as sexual, as seems to be the case with the LGBT community, it is powerful. I discovered this firsthand as I sought to learn sign language and placed myself in situations where the only mode of communication was sign. ASL is its own language with its own sentence structure, vocabulary, and history. But that doesn't fully do it justice. It is a fully embodied language. In English, I can say, "I am angry," but I can use a soft voice, avoid eye contact, cross my arms, tap my foot, or barely articulate the words. When a deaf person signs, "I am angry," the whole body inexorably becomes the vehicle of expression.

I would say that there are virtually no deaf introverts. Following my hunch, I did an online search, and there are actually studies that show that the deaf have much higher extroversion scores. Their "word" is not just a spoken word—either whispered, muttered, declared, or shouted—but a full-bodied expression of their thoughts, their mood, their feelings. Within the Deaf community, in fact, sometimes hearing people are referred to as "robots" for the limited ways they use their bodies. The language itself is not only spatial and temporal, but there is correspondently no adequate way to turn it into a written language. This has profound implications.

> The personality of deaf people was studied within the framework of the Eysenck concept of personality. Data gathered with the Personality Inventory AUPI could be evaluated in 66 deaf people (43 conatal or early acquired deafness, 25 late deafness, i.e. after full language development). The consistency of the AUPI Scales in the normal population about corresponds to that in the deaf people. Those who went deaf "early" showed a statistically significant higher degree of extraversion than the normal population. There was no significant difference in neuroticism (emotional lability).[1]

I see no reason to think there would be significantly different results if this study were done today. My own experience through our work is proof that this is true. It is difficult for people who become hard-of-hearing to keep up communication with hearing people. There are several reasons.
1. For one, they usually deny it, telling people to talk louder. They start to withdraw from social connections, even church, without telling anyone why they do not advocate for themselves, even with their own families.

2. Another reason is that they are not aware of the many technological ways they can hear better, and many of them are unfamiliar with technology. It has been our joy to see the expressions of amazement when a person with severe hearing loss hears through the telecoil for the first time. Their lives are being restored. In my more satiric moments, I tell churchgoers we help a lot more people to hear than Jesus did.

Christological Considerations

I have already alluded to some Christological considerations in the preceding section. To recap here, I believe that how we view the Christ event is crucial to a respectful understanding of "disabled" people, seeing the "disabled" not as broken, needing fixing, or as "other" but as "differently" abled so that their perceived "handicaps," like the wounds of the risen Christ, can transform not only their own lives but the life of the church. I find it fascinating to see how a "high" Christology and a "low" Christology affect marginalized peoples. Much of it relates to where they situate their reward, their redemption.

If, on the one hand, they adhere to a high Christology and perceive their reward as being in the afterlife, where, like the beggar Lazarus in the afterlife parable involving Abraham and the rich man, Lazarus is compensated for his earthly sufferings, this can often paralyze oppressed peoples. They can hold out hope for individual salvation, reunification with predeceased family members, and vindication of their suffering in the eyes of the risen Christ, sitting in all his glory at the right hand of God the Father. Thus, Jesus's short time on earth, abbreviated by an "untimely" death, in the world's shortsighted view, was to show us his uniqueness while pointing the way to a richer afterlife than the one merely endured here on earth. So, instead of working to change oppressive situations that have held them and others down, those focused on the reward of the afterlife merely try to endure as best they can while casting their eyes and hopes heavenward.

If, on the other hand, they adhere to a low Christology, I believe this gives them more leverage for an abundant life now. Jesus who walked among us, laughed with us, cried with us, suffered and triumphed with us, died—as one of us—and ultimately rose, with hands, feet, and side still pierced, is the one I believe offers more hope. If Jesus is like us—as the Unitarian church would put it, "the great example, not the great exception"—then we are to do works of justice and righteousness just as he did, for the kingdom of God is here and now, *both* within us *and* among us.

Additional Issues for the Deaf

Disadvantages of ASL

The main disadvantage for deaf people is that many of them have difficulty understanding written or spoken English because it differs so much from the fluid, manual nature of ASL:

> A group of seventeen- and eighteen-year-old Deaf students studied by Gallaudet researchers in 1997 had a median reading ability at a fourth-grade level. This is not because Deaf people are stupid, but because English is all too often a poorly learned second language to them. The one thing ASL lacks, and it is a *huge* lack, is a written form.[2]

Deaf people are every bit as intelligent as hearing people, but there is an audist assumption about language that values the spoken and written over the manual. This is evident in the attempt to suppress signing acquisition in favor of total oralism. When, for instance, a child receives a cochlear implant at a young age, there is encouragement by the medical community to see the child's deafness as something to be "fixed" rather than an invitation into an additional, rich other community. Concomitantly, schools often do not provide appropriate and adequate support for a deaf child when mainstreamed into the hearing world.

Numerous studies have shown that any child who has the opportunity to be truly bilingual will benefit not only in the acquisition of two languages but also in other areas of studies and learning. Harlan Lane notes that "In his 1986 book summarizing research on bilingualism, psychologist Kenji Hakuta concludes that bilinguals also have an advantage over monolinguals in cognitive flexibility."[3]

Another disadvantage for deaf people is the judgment of hearing people, which takes many forms, some unexpected. For instance, there is a little-known reason and usually overlooked theological implication for the push toward oralism. As has been referred to before, one of the main reasons Thomas Hopkins Gallaudet advocated so strongly for deaf children to be taught sign very early and to be communicated with in sign was that he believed (mistakenly, I hope!) that deaf children needed to be able to form words and thoughts in order to receive the message of salvation.

I found only two books, written in the United Kingdom, that deal specifically and solely with deaf theology, which was not just about how to communicate hearing theology to deaf people but also started from the experiences of deaf people. Even Eiesland's book, *The Disabled God*, has only one passing reference to deafness.[4] Deaf theology per se will be treated below.

Another form of judgment by hearing people is not so much theological as psychological, moral, and aesthetic. This quotation from *An Account of the Origin and Progress of the Pennsylvania Institution of the Deaf and Dumb*, worth quoting again from chapter 9, reveals a theology that, masked in benevolence, inflicts judgment and oppression on the "Deaf and Dumb":

> Idiocy sometimes attendant, often consequent; —the natural powers of the mind exercised to their own perversion or destruction, the passions headstrong and impetuous, by the absence of control of judgement, —fretful impatience at the dark perception of unknown and unattainable excellence in the rest of their species, —the wily cunning of instinct in the place of generous wisdom, —total unfitness for all occupations but those to which the brutes are as well adapted, —an entire and invincible separation from the vast stores of knowledge which human talent has accumulated—ignorance of the truths of Revelation, her glorious assurances and unspeakable consolations, —all these are among the bitter ingredients that fill up the vast measure of affliction to the Deaf and Dumb.[5]

Advantages of ASL and the Attendant Deaf Culture

Even with the difficulties in learning English, being deaf and being in a culturally separate(d) group bring many gifts and blessings. Carol Padden, a deaf student of William Stokoe, who discovered the linguistic underpinnings of ASL, states, "To possess a language that is not quite other languages, yet equal to them, is a powerful realization for a group of people who have long felt their language disrespected and besieged by others' attempts to eliminate it."[6] Michael Chorost, born hard-of-hearing, late-deafened, and a cochlear implant recipient, adds that to "speak ASL is always to be in direct and full contact with the Other. The language binds its speakers together in a community of extraordinary tightness and intimacy."[7]

Chorost also highlights the Deaf community: "Have you ever come into our World? Have you seen us in our everyday lives? Have you ever realized that perhaps being in the Deaf community is a lot more healthy, and that the Deaf community is a more real community than the hearing community is?"[8] Padden adds a final lesson to be learned from the history of Deaf people: "Without diversity of culture, language, and different ways of seeing the world, we would never have learned what we now know about the different ways that humans live. The linguistic and social lives of Deaf people have provided us with unique and valuable ways of exploring the vast potential for human language and culture."[9] She concludes by stating, "Being Deaf was an existential experience, complete in itself and not a consequence of broken bodies but the outcome of biological destiny."[10]

My editor posed these questions here at the end of the chapter: "What about you? Have you benefitted from these advantages of being deaf? Or are you not part of this because of when you lost your hearing?" I had to pause for a long time before I could ferret out some answers. The easy one is "yes and no." On days where I find barriers or have to continue to advocate for myself, it is a hard "no." When I misplace my one, very expensive sound processor and cannot find it immediately, I quickly reach panic, since this is a stark and real reminder that I have only a "visa" to the land of the hearing, a visa that can be revoked at any time with no warning.

Occasionally my hearing loss needs to be taken with a sense of humor. A few months ago, when I arrived at my monthly visit with my spiritual director, I discovered that I had left my hearing device at home. But we forged ahead without a glitch since I had a sound-to-text app on my iPad. When my director asked if I wanted to close my eyes when she prayed, then said she would clap when she was finished, I could not help but laugh. She had not considered that if I did not have my hearing instrument, I would not be able to hear her clap. I still tease her about this today.

Most days, in retrospect, my hearing loss has been a blessing. It introduced me to a unique and special community, which led to my interest in telling their story. It also changed the direction of our shared ministry, so that when Sheryl got ordained several years after me, it became our main focus to advocate and educate around the issues of both the deaf and hard-of-hearing world. If I were told that a new surgery would return my hearing, I think I would probably want it back. It would make my life a lot simpler. Even so, the world I was so suddenly thrust into has been a deeply educational and spiritual journey. It has introduced me to so many people and experiences that I might hesitate a bit before replying.

Notes

[1] G. Savoldelli, abstract from *Archiv für Psychiatrie und Nervenkrankheiten* (Sep 18, 1975): 213–23 [220].

[2] Michael Chorost, *Rebuilt: My Journey Back to the Hearing World* (Mariner Books, 2005), 133, 134.

[3] Harlan Lane, *The Mask of Benevolence: Disabling the Deaf Community* (San Diego, CA: DawnSign Press, 1999), 170.

[4] Nancy L. Eiesland, *The Disabled God: Toward a Liberatory Theology of Disability* (Nashville: Abingdon Press, 1994).

[5] *An Account of the Origin and Progress of the Pennsylvania Institution of the Deaf and Dumb* (Philadelphia: Harvard, 1821).

[6] Carol Padden and Tom Humphries, *Inside Deaf Culture* (Cambridge, MA: Harvard University Press, 2005), 157.

[7] Chorost, *Rebuilt*, 122.

[8] Ibid., 128.

[9] Padden and Humphries, *Inside Deaf Culture*, 180.

[10] Ibid., 157.

Chapter 18
A Theology of The Deaf—
The Work of Wayne Morris and Hannah Lewis

It is interesting how easy the poem "Jabberwocky" by Lewis Carroll is to read. One creates the "slithy toves" and even the Jabberwock out of their own imagination, and yet each person would probably imagine a different one. This is a great example of how, most of the time, I had to imagine my own images, my own conversations, when I lost my hearing. Here are a few lines from Carroll's poem:

> 'Twas brillig, and the slithy toves
> Did gyre and gimble in the wabe;
> All mimsy were the borogoves,
> And the mome raths outgrabe.
> Beware the Jabberwock, my son
> The jaws that bite, the claws that catch![1]

My first MA was in English literature, but try as I might, I still wonder what words such as "slithy," "momgraths," "mimsy," "borogoves," "frablulous," and "uffish" mean. This poem, certainly, is in the realm of whimsy and flights of fancy.

The way we speak to one another to communicate needs to take place on the firm footholds of fully formed, prosaic speech. There are approximately 7,167 living languages across the face of the earth. There is no way anyone can fully learn even a handful of them. And yet someone tried. In 1887, L. L. Zamenhof devised a language as an artificial medium of communication, based on roots from the chief European Languages. The motivation was to create global unity. While we clearly don't all speak Esperanto today, the language has gained more popularity than any other constructed language and continues to attract new speakers. Sometimes speaking Esperanto is written off as a hobby for quirky language people, but it has played pivotal historical roles in the world.

Common words and phrases in Esperanto include bonvenon (welcome), saluton (general greeting of hello), bonan matenon (good morning), pardonu (excuse me), mi petas (please), and dankon (thank you). As I did my research, I wondered if anyone actually uses Esperanto. I then found that the Chinese government has used Esperanto since 2001 for an Esperanto version of its China Internet Information Center. China also uses Esperanto in China Radio International and for the El Popopa Cinio. The Vatican Radio has an Esperanto Version of its podcasts and website. Since I do not plan to go either to Rome or China, I will probably never have a chance to use it.

Most of us will never need this artificial language, yet in the real world of real people, we need to try to communicate with as many others as possible. I believe strongly in what Marlee Matlin said to her hearing partner in *Children of a Lesser God*: "We could find a place not in silence and not in sound."[2] I am willing to find that place. Will you join me?

Introduction

Despite my being a confirmed and addicted bibliophile, I sometimes think too many books have come into print, surely beyond even my overweening, fiendish desire to read them all. Yet, in the field of deaf theology, this is decidedly *not* true. My library and online search uncovered only two books specifically and solely on deaf theology, one in 2007 and the other in 2008, closely following and built largely on the first one. Both books are British, and both are from the Anglican tradition. Thus this chapter is based on two primary sources: first, my own experience and intuitions as a newly deaf person, spending more than a half year in silence before my cochlear implant; and second, a close reading of the two aforementioned books: Wayne Morris's *Theology without Words: Theology in the Deaf Culture*[3] and Hannah Lewis's *Deaf Liberation Theology*.[4]

"In the Beginning Was the "Word": The Inescapable and Primary Problem of Language

The Hebrew Scriptures start in Genesis with the words, "In the beginning…, God said…" (Gen 1:1, 3, NIV). John's Gospel begins with the words, "In the Beginning was the Word [*Logos*], and the Word was with God, and the Word was God" (John 1:1, NIV). Almost anyone within a biblical tradition is familiar with these two passages. Yet how can such a seemingly inoffensive term like "Word" become oppressive, specifically for born deaf people who do not have "words" as we understand them?

Although the concept of *Logos* can be and has been expanded, it is easy to conflate its nuanced meanings into a Hellenistic model linked with perceiving God in God's essence as a reasoning intellectual being whom we, as human beings, the "crown" of creation, must mirror to be part of the *Imago Dei* (image of God), which has come to be limited to those who use speech and a written language. At the now infamous Congress of Milan in 1880, where oralism won out and began almost a century of systematic suppression of manualism, signing was considered to be "devil-inspired nonsense."[5] Guilio Tarra, at the same conference, said, "Oral speech is the sole power that can rekindle the light God breathed into man when, giving him a soul in a corporeal body, he gave him also a means of understanding, of conceiving and of expression."[6] We also unthinkingly call the Bible "the Word of God" and use an oral, word-centered preaching event as central to common liturgy.

Many deaf people do not speak at all and have varying degrees of difficulty relating either to spoken or written English. And not only is ASL decidedly *not* English, but there is also not yet—and possibly will never be—a written form of sign language. Deaf culture is non-literary, based in a storytelling tradition literally handed down in signs from one generation to another. "Oral" is, for obvious reasons, not a word that can be accurately used in the teaching of sign, but it does have much in common with oral traditions from other cultures (more on that in the next section). Deaf theology, as Wayne Morris writes, is lived:

> …it is temporary and not fixed for "eternity," in written creeds or in texts…but is based on reflective experience expressed through BSL [British Sign Language—we can substitute ASL, American Sign language, here], relevant to a particular moment in history…. Because Deaf culture is a non-literary culture…they are excluded from many of the sources of Christian theology as the Bible, Church tradition, and modern theological research.[7]

Morris summarizes by stating that "…the Bible is problematic as a source of the language and images it uses about God."[8]

Oral Tradition Versus Signing

While it is linguistically and politically incorrect and insensitive to refer to deaf tradition as an "oral" tradition since it is conveyed and handed down in sign rather than speech, it is valuable to revisit the practice and theology of oral traditions, both in the past and now in the present. Western academics are immersed in books. They are cheap and readily available. Libraries and bookstores abound. The internet has made much previously printed material available at the stroke of a computer key. That was not so for most of human history.

> By 1424, Cambridge University library owned only 122 books—each of which had a value equal to a farm or vineyard. The demand for these books was driven by rising literacy amongst the middle class and students in Western Europe. At this time, the Renaissance was still in its early stages and the populace was gradually removing the monopoly the clergy had held on literacy.[9]

Then along came Gutenberg's printing press, invented in 1439, which fueled the Protestant Reformation ignited by Martin Luther in 1517. The Reformation led quickly to the Age of Reason, followed by the Age of Enlightenment, the nineteenth-century Industrial Revolution, the rise of literacy rates and public education, and now, the invention and widespread availability of computers and the World Wide Web. We tend to think that God and theology have come along as passengers, perhaps unwilling, in this technological explosion of knowledge. We forget the long and valuable tradition of non-written forms of communication not only in our own past but still in many parts of the world today.

One does not need much of a classical education to remember that Homer's *Odyssey* and *Iliad* were crafted and performed orally. Bards and troubadours roved around Europe carrying their tales and songs in their heads and hearts, not in their knapsacks. Mystery and morality plays were performed without written scripts or manual aids. People gathered around campfires, in country inns, or at a peasant family's wooden table to be entertained, to rejoice, to remember.

More recently, much of liberation theology has focused on the oral traditions of Indigenous peoples, both to be appropriately subversive of and to expand on purely literary texts and interpretations. Alan Dundes's book *Holy Writ as Oral Lit* investigates the oral precedents of the written texts of the Bible, using his understanding of folklore to help explain variant biblical passages. A number of theologians have worked with oral traditions and Christian faith, including African theologians such as Canaan Banana and Mercy Amba Oduyoye. Dalit theology in India is largely oral. This is where deaf theology intersects: "The written word is an abstract thing. The spoken [or signed] word is an event."[10]

Medical Model, Social Model, or New Cultural Model?

Before we address the Bible's treatment of the disabled, specifically stories surrounding the healing of deaf people and their segregation from worship because of their ritual impurity, it is necessary to revisit the model used in this chapter.

Medical Model

To recap, in the medical model, the child is seen outside a social context, where deafness is simply a medical problem that can be remediated. Wayne Morris writes in *Theology without Words*,

> The medical model's goal is one in which it is assumed to be ethically right that the Deaf child is enabled to be as much like a hearing child as possible.... Playing on those parents' fears of "abnormality" and their desire to achieve "normality," they (proponents of the medical approach) then present their medical model which claims that normality can only be achieved by denying the realities of deafness and keeping their children away from Deaf communities lest they be "contaminated" by them. The quest for a

cure for Deafness has both historically and in contemporary society had negative consequences for Deaf children.[11]

Morris concludes by saying that the "desire for a cure for Deaf people has had devastating, at times, fatal consequences for Deaf people throughout history. In contemporary situations, the desire for cure of Deaf people by hearing people continues."[12]

Social Model
Morris likes the social model a bit more since it puts the "blame" on society and the responsibility for ameliorating the "plight" of the deaf person on the institution rather than the individual, but he still finds fault with it. The social model's flaws are still defining the deaf only by their having a medical problem and by thinking that somehow, if society but tries hard enough, it can virtually "erase" all the barriers deaf—and other "disabled" minorities—must face daily. This model defines the deaf as having a medical problem but simply tries to minimize it. Morris concludes, however, that

> Contrary to popular opinion, disabled people and non-disabled people cannot do everything they set their minds to; all must live with and accept that certain limitations, other than social ones, are placed on their lives and that limitation itself can be a source of creativity. The social model aims to achieve greater equality in society by recognizing the social barriers that limit disabled people from participating in society equally.[13]

New Cultural Model
Morris's new cultural model, based on the work done by disabled people and the World Health Organization, claims that a new approach is needed that brings together the two perspectives of the medical and social models. This approach would involve respecting disabled people as human beings with their own unique gifts and abilities. It would also accept that

> …social barriers suppress the ability of many disabled people to participate fully in society. It would recognize that medical intervention can be useful for many disabled people. Choice and freedom are paramount. This new approach would also recognize that disabled people are a diverse group of people, and no single model is realistically applicable to all.[14]

Morris claims that the full inclusion of deaf people in the larger society will not be accomplished by all the technological gimmicks, such as flashing doorbells, text messengers, captioned phones, or even having sign language interpreters on duty at every public event. Inclusion will come about only when there is "a more fundamental transformation in the perception of Deafness in society and the response that emerges from that."[15] He further claims that deaf people's experience is actually a dual oppression: the first from being a cultural-linguistic minority group whose legitimacy of language is just being recognized and the second from being a disabled group whom society believes should be "normalized" as much as possible.

Let us take this third model, the new model of a paradigm for deafness and deaf people, into our treatment of deaf people and the Bible. A transformation will have to happen in this severely constricted "Word of God" to allow deaf people to find a place there where they can stand proudly in their full, healed, and holy personhood.

Deaf People and the Bible: Problems and Transformation

Some theologians, such as Hannah Lewis, an Anglican priest post-lingually deafened in childhood, still believe that the Bible itself is redeemable:

> It is possible to argue that the Bible is irredeemably anti-Deaf, written by hearing people for hearing people and only including Deaf people as passive objects for controlling, or negative subjects for elimination. However, this approach ignores the history of the Bible as a liberating text for many minorities, not least Deaf people in history. It also assumes that there is only one meaning to be found in any text, an assumption that is difficult to defend in a post-modern worldview.[16]

Fernando Segovia (add footnote below to Segovia) tries to redeem something, however, by directly addressing the underlying, usually unacknowledged issues (at least by those oppressed by the "sacred" texts). He claims that "postcolonial Bible study needs to renounce the idea of a 'master narrative' itself as a construct and take the diversity of texts, readers and readings to heart as well as recognizing the reality of imperialism and colonialism in both ancient and contemporary times."[17] As we explore issues related to the entire appropriation of the Bible for deaf people, we now have some context. Wayne Morris raises a number of issues, all of which deserve at least a line or two.

Deaf People's Alienation from the Bible
Morris examines several important primary texts in the Bible that deaf people look at with different eyes. For instance, how would a deaf person view the encounter with God (Exodus 3:1-6) that Moses had at the burning bush? Since no one could look at God directly and live, God turned God's back on Moses, who then needed to rely on his ears to hear the Lord. It's a good thing Moses wasn't deaf! Not being

able to encounter God face to face means the deaf are de facto excluded from the intimacy due to their inability to hear.

In the Hebrew Scriptures, in Leviticus 21:16-23, the deaf are impure and cannot fully participate in Temple service. In the Christian Scriptures, Mark 7:32-37 is the story of Jesus healing a deaf person (NRSV):

> They brought to him [Jesus] a deaf man who had an impediment in his speech, and they begged him to lay his hand on him. He took him aside in private, away from the crowd, and put his fingers into his ears, and he spat and touched his tongue. Then looking up to heaven, he sighed and said to him, "Ephphatha," that is, "Be opened." And his ears were opened, his tongue was released, and he spoke plainly. Then Jesus ordered them to tell no one, but the more he ordered them, the more zealously they proclaimed it. They were astounded beyond measure, saying, "He has done everything well; he even makes the deaf to hear and the mute to speak."

Morris points out some intriguing ways that this passage can be made more "palatable" to the Deaf community. For instance, Jesus does not rely solely on the spoken word for this particular healing but uses an intimate touch to heal the man. The word "Ephphatha" is one that someone relying on lip reading could readily make out. Also, from a deaf standpoint, the miracle is not so much that the deaf man's ears are opened but that someone previously "dumb," without sound, is now able to speak plainly, having presumedly never heard speech before.

In John's Gospel, when questioned by his disciples about the "reason" for a man being blind, Jesus answers, "Neither this man nor his parents sinned; he was born blind so that God's works might be revealed in him" (John 9:3, NRSV). We might also apply this to the deaf. Yet Morris states that this is not enough because curing the deafness, no matter the perceived "cause" of the condition, can be problematic:

> Most born Deaf people, however, do not see becoming hearing as something they wish for. They believe that their cultural identity, which Deafness gives them, forms a part of who they are and to lose their Deafness would be to become a different person beyond recognition. Some Deaf people have also informed me that they would not particularly want to be hearing in heaven either. The Deaf experience and some biblical perspectives on Deafness are sometimes miles apart.[18]

He goes on to talk about deaf people's difficulty relating to the Holy Spirit. If the two primary ways deaf people relate, sight and touch, are taken away, then what is left? Even the language of prayer, "Hear our prayer," is problematic for deaf people. Morris asks if there is anything in the Bible that *can* be for deaf people.

Hope for the Deaf in the Bible

Morris does manage to find some hope in the Bible. For instance, he cites the oft-repeated phrase, "Lift up your hands." This is appropriate for deaf people, for using their hands is their language of prayer. Another issue is a question deaf people ask: "Does God have a body?" This feeds into the body-soul dualism I have already addressed. The more incarnate, the more touchable and seeable, God is, the better the ability to connect with deaf people.

Theology without the Bible?

This is an intriguing idea. We are often so wedded to the text, especially in highly liturgical traditions that rely on the lectionary, that the very notion of theology without the Bible might seem at least a major loss if not outright scandalous. This is compounded by the more fundamentalist traditions that have turned the "inerrant" Bible, where they believe the written words have the "exact" words of God recorded for all eternity, into their only source of faith. Yet speech and sign language, the oral tradition itself, managed for millennia to share culture, values, and religious experiences. The canonical Gospels took between forty and sixty years to settle into a written text from collections of oral traditions such as "Q" that were handed on verbally from group to group.

Alternative Understandings on How to Use the Bible

Here Morris cites the Zimbabwean Methodist theologian, Canaan Banana, who argued that the Bible not only needs editing but that the canon itself should be reopened for other texts, including contemporary ones. Banana served as the first president of Zimbabwe from 1980 to 1987 and was known for his involvement in the Zimbabwean liberation struggle and his contributions to the development of the new nation. Morris also refers to Peter Kalilombe, a Malawian and pioneering theologian and ecclesiologist who stated that the Bible should be read aloud and also transmitted the way the Qur'an is transmitted. Then he reiterated the feminist stance that the Bible is useful only if it affirms the worth and identity of women and extended this concept specifically to the dialogue that needs to happen between deaf people and the Bible.[19]

This reminds me of the way Jesus answered his antagonists, who tried to trap him when they asked him about his disciples breaking one of the many Sabbath laws. Jesus said, "The Sabbath was made for humankind and not humankind for the Sabbath" (Mark 2:27, NRSVue). When we "worship" the Bible as the firmly fixed, eternal, rigid, and definitive "Word" of God, are we not placing the Bible before the needs of people seeking a liberatory message, no matter what form it might take?

Lewis goes further into uncovering the underpinnings of a colonial theology that, she convincingly argues, has no place in a postmodernist world:

> Aspects of post-modernism that are particularly significant in this process of liberation of theology include the understanding that knowledge is subjective or contextual, constructed and can be used as an instrument of power. The identification of all knowledge, all readings of the text and interpretations of events and behavior as partial, seen through the lenses of our own contexts and backgrounds, has had huge implications for minority groups, including Deaf people—people who have been told for years that others (white, middle-class, western, academic men) know, better than they do, what is right for them.[20]

She goes on to say that interpretations of all events, even the central "Christ-event" that is the foundation of Christian theology, are partial and subjective, suggesting that for any theology to be universal or relevant outside its immediate context is questionable, to say the least. There is no longer a place where we can speak of one right, unchanging theology.

Then Lewis specifically addresses the deaf experience of theology, where one barrier in the past has been the perception that to be academically valid and taken seriously, knowledge must be written down in a logical format. However, in postmodern times, this criterion has been recognized as a means of power exercised by an educational elite group over minorities. Postmodernism "has recognized 'oral' or 'signed' knowledge as a valid form of knowledge production."[21]

Deaf Use of the Bible and "Reading the Gaps"

Regarding deaf use of the Bible, Morris cites the work of Chinese feminist theologian, Kwok Pui-lan, who writes about experiences of non-literate women when they dramatize the Bible and add their own stories and questions.[22] He adds the new work of Visible Communications in the United Kingdom, which is an organization working to translate stories from the Bible into British Sign Language. Then he speaks of dramatizing the Bible and "reading the gaps," which means that the ones interacting with the story can add their own questions and personal experiences, so that they are not just "receiving" the text but integrating it into their own lives.

Conclusion: Deaf Theology and the Bible

Morris concludes that, for all the reasons cited above, for many deaf people the Bible is problematic in terms of its language and imagery as well as because it is a written text. On the plus side, he states that some of the language for God used in the Bible is more inclusive of deaf people, most notably the theologies that point towards an incarnational Christology. This is because the incarnation tells of a God who is both visible and tangible. Yet deaf people often do with the Bible the opposite of what hearing people have done with it:

> Rather than beginning with oral traditions and writing them down, Deaf people have familiarized themselves with the narratives in the Bible and in order to make them useful, they are turned back into oral or signing traditions using drama and the "reading the gaps" method of engaging with biblical narratives. Their theology is informed by using the Bible in this way and their reading of the Bible is informed by their theological perspectives and experiences.[23]

Ecclesiology Overview

Morris prefers the term "Deaf Church" rather than "Sign Language Church" because it has more implications and deeper meanings. All too often, the "hearing" church thinks that just providing an ASL interpreter is enough to be fully inclusive. Yet a Deaf Church is not just "for" deaf people in a patronizing way but includes deaf people in all leadership positions, and the liturgy, as well as the sacred space, comes from the experiences of deaf people.

The space itself, for instance, would be well lit, showing not only the speaker's hands and head but full body. The seats would be in tiers to make sure everyone has a clear line of sight. It would be better if the seats were in the round, to permit deaf people to more easily interact with one another. Hearing people would be welcome, but not in positions of leadership. In terms of the actual liturgy, one must keep in mind the original meaning of the liturgy as a "work of the people." Thus, it does not have to be book-centered but needs to be experience-centered. The passing of the peace and intercessory prayers, for instance, could be spontaneous, shared, leading to visiting and storytelling, and including lots of physical contact beyond token bows or handshakes.

The written texts would still remain problematic, even when projected on screens. The sermon needs to be informal, allowing people to ask questions and share personal experiences. Morris even predicts that music itself will disappear in the Deaf Church. It is virtually impossible to coordinate signing with the tempo of music, especially if the signer is using the native structure of signing rather than a word-for-word translation of English.

Morris ends this section by fleshing out three approaches to creating a truly deaf liturgy. The first one relies on translating or interpreting the hearing texts. The next level is translating with cultural sensitivity, replacing, for instance, "Hear our prayer" with something like "Receive our prayer." "Sing to the Lord," along the same vein, would be rendered "Sign to the Lord."

The third approach, the one he advocates, gives the project over to deaf people themselves, so instead of others doing "for" them, they take charge of their own worship experience. This approach has yet to be fully fleshed out because it requires the "colonizing" powers of audist theologians and liturgists, even with the best intentions, to move aside, sit down, and shut up.

Morris, himself hearing, proclaims that "A truly Deaf liturgy will only ever be achieved by Deaf people having the freedom to create and express worship in ways that emerge from Deaf culture and experience."[24] To do this, deaf people need to stand up against received authority and claim their own, one based on their own history, preserved and handed down through often forbidden signs from one generation of deaf to the next.

Deaf in the Image of the Deaf God

I have already written at length about Nancy Eiesland's book, *The Disabled God*. Here I want to narrow the disability specifically to deafness. I alluded to it in the section above on the Bible and deafness and some alternative exegeses that see the deaf person as whole, rather than broken.

Wayne Morris begins by quoting Matthew 5:48: "Be perfect, therefore, as your heavenly Father is perfect" (NIV). He then asks the question, "What is perfection?" He starts literally at the beginning, by quoting from Genesis 1:27, the priestly account of creation, where the sacred text declares that "So God created humankind in his [sic] image" (NRSVue). This is the paradisical paradigm. Then there is the expulsion from the garden, millennia of wandering about, and finally Jesus declaring anew in Matthew 5, "Be perfect, therefore, as your heavenly Father is perfect."

Morris then speaks of the Orthodox tradition of the *ikon*, not simply a two-dimensional artistic portrayal of some saint or other but "a creation towards the Divine: icons fulfill a 'sacramental function, constituting a channel of divine grace… the icon acts as a point of meeting, a place of encounter.'"[25] Of this image, he says,

> Whether humans are already made as *ikons* of God or they are striving to be *ikons* of God (perhaps a mixture of the two), I suggest that these two strands are part of the same tradition of connecting the Divine with humans and recognizing that in some way the human form points beyond

itself towards God. But what does such a notion mean for a person who is Deaf, especially that of being *ikons* which are striving to be perfect like their heavenly Father?[26]

He then examines three areas of concern relating to this concept of the possibility of deaf people representing the ikon of perfection.

1. Deafness, Perfection, and Sin

Morris claims that, while some still believe deafness is individual punishment for sin, that interpretation doesn't withstand critique. "It is arguable that if Deafness itself can in any way be viewed as having the potential to be positive and creative," he writes, "then the experiences of many Deaf people suggests that Deafness is not some awful punishment but a part of the creative intentions of a loving God."[27]

2. Deafness and Physical Perfection

Morris declares that in the Western world, "perfection" is not only interpreted as being without sin but is also seen in terms of physical beauty and strength. This idea is even harder to fight against. We can see it enacted in the holiness codes of the Hebrew Scriptures. More recently, it has been used to exclude otherwise qualified candidates from ordained ministry in the Catholic Church into an instrument of oppression towards deaf people.

This attitude is evident in a discussion on genetic engineering for deafness. The point of view is shared by a number of geneticists who claim that deaf people do not have a right not to "cure" their children since there is technology, such as a cochlear implant, to eradicate deafness. A great many deaf people interpret this a way to simply erode deaf culture. I would direct the reader to watch the two videos listed in the bibliography, *The Sound and the Fury*, to see how a deaf family initially refuses to have their young daughter get a cochlear implant. In the second film, not only has she received one, but so have her deaf mother and two brothers.

Morris, however, strongly disagrees, concluding, "Not only must Deaf people not be understood as being punished for sin and therefore lesser *ikons* of God, but in addition, the concept of perfection, in the light of the Gospel itself, needs to be re-interpreted in contra-distinction to Western cultural notions of perfection being about physical prowess, intellectual abilities or social success."[28]

3. Being Perfect: Deaf People as *Ikons* of God

Here Morris does an exegesis of the Greek word τέλειος, usually translated imperfectly as "perfect," means not a static, Platonic perfection but to "bring to perfection" or to "complete." Thus, it is a task that *all* of us are called to, and he claims that the "forces which stop people being fulfilled or complete are the forces of evil taking humanity away from being *ikons* of the Father, because they oppress and marginalize people and are thus contrary to the will of God who desires that his people are *teleios* just like himself."[29]

Is God Deaf?

A number of theologians, working from varying liberation perspectives, have wrested God from the white, male, Western, colonial pedestal on which so much of orthodox theology has rested. "God is Black." "God is female." "God is gay." The theology behind this is that, if God cannot be somehow viscerally connected to different groups of oppressed peoples, then of what earthly use is God?

James Cone, famed, or considered by some notorious, African American theologian, claims that while God is beyond all categories, God must also *always* take a stand with the oppressed, not just as a decolonized liberator but as one of the oppressed. He states that "There is no place in black theology for a colorless God in a society where human beings suffer precisely because of their colour."[30] As uncomfortable as it may be for some people to perceive a Black God, Morris says "there is still undoubtedly even greater discomfort when anyone talks about God as Deaf, disabled, limited, vulnerable, and broken. Nevertheless, this is the starting point at which Deaf and Disabled people are remythologizing the Christian tradition in terms of their own context."[31]

This is absolutely essential. Lewis summarizes the idea succinctly: "[A]sking God to cure me of my deafness is comparable to asking God to make me a man."[32] Being deaf is not so much a limitation as it is an invitation—to experience both oneself and God in a new, certainly different, and perhaps even deeper way.

The Deaf God

Do deaf people envision a God who is physically like them, deaf like them? Probably most do not. Yet they can and do experience a deaf God in that, as Lewis writes,

> …many Deaf people understand their Deafness as much more than… simply being biologically unable to hear. It also includes being part of a culture. Consequently, in the Deaf community there is a strong sense… that God is culturally Deaf, and I would suggest that for Deaf people, this is far more important in their thinking than the idea of God as being unable to hear in a physical sense. This is demonstrated primarily through the way Deaf people sign about their experience of God, their understanding of Jesus from the Gospel narratives and other stories about God in the Bible, and how God is presented when those stories are told about him in BSL [read ASL].[33]

Again, as stated above, Jesus, in healing the man born deaf, relates to him as a person and communicates with him directly and appropriately, understanding the ways he can reach out to touch him. But we need to go, yet again, even further. We need to understand and affirm that the *Imago Dei* to which we have alluded, the *ikon* of God, applies to deaf people not in their potential, either here or in the afterlife, for hearing but as deaf people here, now, fully complete, fully whole and holy. M. K. Weir says that "…to be made in the image of God is to live as the body of God in all its diversity: 'not just males, certainly not just able-bodied people, but all human beings reflect God.'"[34]

My Personal Reflections

While I am no means an "instant" expert, my initially unwilling total immersion into the Deaf experience, extending from May 22, 2008, when I woke up in the hospital totally deaf three days after total knee replacement surgery, to December 15 of the same year, when I was "activated" for sound following cochlear implant surgery, my seven-month deaf immersion experience gave me much time and inclination to ponder the theological implications of becoming deaf. As I healed and read and meditated and studied, several strands of thought began to weave through my personal deaf experience, some of which I share here.

Scriptural Words Reexamined

I believe some words from both Greek and Hebrew need revisiting and deeper study. I have already written about the damage a narrow interpretation of *Logos* can do. Concomitantly, the word *dabar* in the Hebrew scriptures, usually just translated "word," also means "deed," which is not limited to the spoken word. *Sophia* too, the divine emanation of Wisdom in the Hebrew scriptures, is the one who inhabits the Song of Solomon, the creation hymns in Job, the Proverbs.

Both *nefesh* and *ruah* also offer expansive interpretations. *Nefesh* means "living being" and is sometimes translated as "neck," the place through which the lifeblood flows—the blood that could not be consumed but just returned to the earth when an animal was slaughtered. Since blood was the essence of life, it could not be eaten but was instead reserved for the priests, who returned it to God by pouring it on the altar (Leviticus 17:10-16). Consumption of meat could only happen in this ritual context since the killing of a permitted (kosher) animal required proper disposal of the blood.

This essence of life is living, flowing, and constantly going out and returning, like the life of the Spirit. It is similar to *ruah*, "spirit" or "breath," which also corresponds to the intake and expulsion of air. A theology of *nefesh*, coupled with the work of God as experienced through the "breath," the *ruah*, would closely approximate the lived experience the deaf would bring to the Bible and to liturgy, one in which a closed, rigid canon would spell death, not life.

Telling the Biblical Stories without Words

While I lost my hearing as a post-lingually deaf person, I was born, raised, and educated in the hearing world. Much of my theorizing and pondering is still done one step removed from the experience of being born and raised deaf. Yet, as I read and prayed, it occurred to me that perhaps many, if not most, theologically educated people, me among them, had placed too much emphasis on the spoken or written word. I wondered if it would be possible to "tell" the major events of salvation history, especially those in the Christian scriptures, without the readily available, but as I now view it equally reductionist, written words.

I could easily imagine events such as the birth narratives, the baptism, the temptation in the desert, the Last Supper with its blessings of bread and wine, the anointing with oil of Jesus prior to his death, the foot washing, the Via Dolorosa, the crucifixion, and indeed the resurrection and ascension all expressed without words. The Seven Signs of John's Gospel could also be shared without words:

- The First Sign: Turning Water into Wine at Cana
- The Second Sign: The Healing of the Nobleman's Son
- The Third Sign: The Healing of the Palsied Man
- The Fourth Sign: The Feeding of the Five Thousand
- The Fifth Sign: The Storm on the Lake and Jesus Walking on the Sea
- The Sixth Sign: The Healing of the Blind Man
- The Seventh Sign: The Raising of Lazarus from Death

Many people, not just Christians, know Jesus by his parables, as a number of them have passed into popular language. While they are *related* in speech, they are not told linearly but are couched in imagination. They are stories, not creeds or discursive reasoning. They would adapt easily to deaf culture, to the right side of our brains, where logic and reasoning have no toehold.

For me, the highest example is in John's Gospel, chapter 20, when the resurrected Jesus, translucent perhaps—certainly so different that the disciples are barely able to recognize him—shows them his hands and feet and wounded side. Thomas alone has the courage to reach out and touch him. Jesus's "perfect" body has not erased the wounds of his suffering and death but transformed them. Deaf people are people of touch who need to verify, to claim their experience, not through a sense of hearing that doesn't exist but through a sense of touching in which they dare to reach out and put their hands in the side of the risen, yet still somehow wounded, Christ, realizing that both they and he are whole—and always have been.

The Underlying Theology of Some Deaf Signs

While I am by no means an ASL expert, having completed only one course, my attempt to learn sign language has revealed to me some interesting ideas about an underlying and inchoate "theology" of sign language. I put the word "theology" in quotes because it is something that is naturally flowing, if not unconscious then certainly subconscious. I have neither the time nor the competence to fully explore this issue, but I do have some preliminary thoughts about several signs.

- *sign for Jesus*: Middle finger of one hand touches palm of other hand, then they reverse, indicating the stigmata
- *sign for worship*: Mimicking swinging of a censer
- *liturgy*: Mimicking swinging of a censer, followed by the sign for processing
- *sign for "deaf"*: Touches both ear and mouth with index finger, even if deaf person can speak, so means both deaf and speechless
- *sign for "hearing"*: Index finger, held horizontally, makes small, closed circles in front of lips, indicating not that a person can hear but that a hearing person can speak
- *sign for Holy Spirit*: Middle finger and thumb touch palm of one hand, then rise in a small spiral
- *sign for life*: The "L" handshape of both hands begins at the stomach and rises to the shoulders, indicating "living" as movement upwards rather than a static, stationary sign
- *heal*: Fingers of open hands touch chest, then come forward into fists, a sign of "power"

These signs can point to a living, breathing, incarnational theology that will not, indeed *cannot*, be confined in a canon, in written symbols fixed for all eternity on paper, their symbols clear, constant, and unmoving. They flow—like life itself—reaching outward and upward, pulsing on the continually renewing living breath of Spirit. This is deaf theology.

As I reflected on the journey we have all taken together in this book, a poem I wrote while in the hospital after my knee surgery, where I was stuck in bed and isolated from everyone else in the darkness due to my sudden deafness. I believe it has a lesson for us all as we ponder the stories and ideas in this book.

People travel to keep from crying in one place
Mary Heron Dyer

It has been said that people travel
to keep from crying in one place,
but sometimes that's not a choice…
Right now, they'd have to take me on a gurney
or a coffin, if it comes to that…
Like a specimen moth,
pierced and mounted in a display case
for someone else's pleasure,
I am not once but doubly pinned to this place,
a hospital bed in the East Bay,
the Golden Gates beckoning yet far away,
tantalizingly beyond my reach
on this shimmering soft day.
First pinned by an old knee who had done its devotions for me, the new
one learning its job;
and the second unexpected metaphysical "twist,"
a sudden onset and inexplicable hearing loss,
throwing me without warning or caution
into a chasm of silence.
Leaving deafness aside, a bubbly young man,
with gangly, youthful legs as yet untried by
life's uncertain terrain,
where the very land itself shifts underneath
the more seasoned traveler's uncertain feet,
strides into my room,
challenging me to mount the concrete
stairs with a walker.
As we toe the line,
leaning towards the imaginary pistol's flare,
in such an unpaired race,
his coltish legs easily straddle the width of the steps,
his young knees leap with grace and ease from step to step,
like a young foal enticing its mother to the summer pasture,
his still-greenstick legs testing the mettle of the meadow
against his fresh-minted hooves,
eager for the larger world.
Moments later, tired but strangely triumphant,

and having treated myself to a ride down the elevator,
I offer myself again to the clean white sheets,
embrace of well-earned rest,
to the constraint of the still unfamiliar
and ill-fitting garment of outer silence.
Pinned again against my bed tonight,
the weight of double darkness presses me down
into the depths of my own despair,
neither sight nor sound to interrupt my
darkening mood.
I have no choice but to cry in this one place.

As beautiful as a moth specimen is, it is dead, pinned to be put on display to show its beauty, whereas its real beauty can only be experienced in flight or when it lands on a flower to taste the nectar. Wanting to "pin" things in place is a strong tendency for us. We long for stability, for security, for certainty. We see how this brought about the various creeds of the emerging church, scriptural quotes wrapped up in dogmas. But moths, scripture, and binary descriptions of people all need to be freed, to continue flying, taking us to beautiful places we never even imagined. My sincere hope is that this book has freed you from the chains of trying to define, categorize, and dominate both LGBT people and deaf people. Only then can the "Wholly Other" become the "Holy Other."

Is the Apostle's Creed Truly Inclusive?

Until I delved more deeply into this issue, I had just assumed that this ancient creed, over which theological wars were fought, was truly inclusive for all believers. The Deaf community disagrees, exposing its essence as a hearing and spoken document de facto excluding those who identify as deaf.

Hannah Lewis, an Anglican priest from England, was not born deaf but lost her hearing very young. In her book, *Deaf Liberation Theology*, Lewis develops a creed that specifically highlights both the difference from the hearing and the ways this creed has, albeit probably unintentionally, excluded those who are deaf.

Following years of theology of deafness based on the premise that deaf people are simply people who cannot hear, this book breaks new ground. It allows deaf people who see themselves as members of a minority group to formulate their own theology rooted in their own history and culture. Lewis deconstructs the ancient creed to prove that the Church, for millennia, has been oppressing deaf people by simply defining them only as those who cannot hear. She then goes on to scrutinize this ancient text to read it through the eyes of a deaf person.

In this book, I have already discussed how those who were born deaf were taken away from their families, put into deaf schools, and were not allowed to use sign language. The entire emphasis was put on teaching them to lip read and to speak, to be able to sort of "pass" in the hearing world. A sterling example of this is Helen Keller, whose ability to do those things allowed her to travel all over the world with her companion Annie Sullivan. In addition to depriving the deaf from communicating effectively among themselves, some so-called "Christian" theology believed that their deafness made them unfit for heaven.

Thus, deaf creeds challenge the spoken creed with language claiming that God made them, full deaf, but still in the image of God, just as "perfect" and worthy as their hearing pew mates. Their being deaf was not a mistake, not a way to isolate them in life and condemn them to hell in the afterlife. This creed goes on to say Jesus' death and resurrection freed them from the bondage of oppression and of a world that wants them to pretend to be hearing. And the beauty of sign language speaks to the very depths of their soul.

This understanding would be incomprehensible to me as a formerly hearing person. I had been deaf for seven months, during which time I was busily trying to learn ASL at Berkeley Community College. I was taking a preaching class at American Baptist Seminary, part of the Graduate Theological Union in Berkeley, California. I was the only deaf person in class, although I had received a cochlear implant by that time. It was still very hard to keep up with the class. Both the professor and students had to be taught to speak directly into a microphone so that I could hear more clearly through my telecoil setting.

When my time came to speak, I decided to give them a small taste of the deaf world. I had the lights turned off and stood next to a lit candle. I signed a favorite Psalm to them, signing a verse then having Sheryl repeat it in words, then kept on going like this through the whole Psalm. It was the first time I had prayed in sign, using my entire body to incarnate it. It was such a great feeling to not just use the words from by mouth, but create them from the expressions of my face, the movement of my body, the use of my hands. I was fully alive.

Notes

[1] Read the whole nonsense poem at *Poetry Foundation*: https://www.poetryfoundation.org/poems/42916/jabberwocky.

[2] *Children of a Lesser God*, based on 1979 play by Mark Medoff, screenplay by Medoff and Hesper Anderson, directed by Randa Haines, Paramount Pictures, 114 minutes, 1986.

[3] Wayne Morris, *Theology without Words: Theology in the Deaf Community* (Hampshire, England: Ashgate, 2008).

[4] Hannah Lewis, *Deaf Liberation Theology* (Aldershot, England: Ashgate, 2007).

[5] A. F. Dimmock, *Cruel Legacy: An Introduction to the Record of Deaf People in History*, (Edinburgh: Scottish Workshop Publications, 1993), 18, quoted in Lewis, *Deaf Liberation Theology*, 82.

[6] In Harlan Lane, *When the Mind Hears: A History of the Deaf* (New York: Vintage Books, 1989).

[7] Morris, *Theology without Words*, xv.

[8] Ibid., xvi.

[9] "Printing press," *Wikipedia*, http://en.wikipedia.org/wiki/Printing_press.

[10] Alan Dundes, *Holy Writ as Oral Lit: The Bible as Folklore* (Lanham, MD: Rowman and Littlefield, Publishers, Inc., 1999), 70, 71.

[11] Morris, *Theology without Words*, 70, 71.

[12] Ibid., 9.

[13] Ibid., 70, 71.

[14] Ibid., 8.

[15] Ibid., 11.

[16] Lewis, *Deaf Liberation Theology*, 107.

[17] Ibid., 109. Quote from Fernando F. Segovia, *Decolonizing Biblical Studies: A View from the Margins* (Maryknoll, NY: Orbis, 2020).

[18] Morris, *Theology without Words*, 99.

[19] See Patrick A. Kalilombe, *Doing Theology at the Grassroots: Theological Essays from the Grassroots* (Malawi: Luviri Press, 2008).

[20] Lewis, *Deaf Liberation Theology*, 5.

[21] Ibid.

[22] Kwok Pui-lan, *The Anglican Tradition from a Postcolonial Perspective* (White Plains, NT: Seabury Books, 2023).

[23] Morris. *Theology without Words*, 110, 111.

[24] Ibid., 134.

[25] Ibid., 138, quoting K. Ware, "The Spirituality of the Icon," in C. Jones et al., eds., *The Study of Spirituality* (London: Oxford University Press, 2000), 197.

[26] Ibid., 137.

[27] Ibid., 138.

[28] Ibid., 139.

[29] Ibid., 140.

[30] James Cone, *A Black Theology of Liberation: Twentieth Anniversary Edition* (Maryknoll, NY: Orbis, 1990), 63.

[31] Morris, *Theology without Words*, 141.

[32] Lewis, *Deaf Liberation Theology*, 1.

[33] Ibid., 148.

[34] M. K. Weir, "Made Deaf in God's Image," in International Ecumenical Working Group, *The Place of Deaf People in the Church* (Northampton, 1996), 6, as cited in Morris, *Theology without Words*, 46.

Conclusion
An Epistemology of Hope

I have covered much ground in these pages. I began by speaking of the human impulse, when encountering an "Other," to either try to assimilate them or annihilate them. Then I held up the work of both Levinas and Thurman to offer a place where we can lay aside our fears to meet the "Other" face to face on holy ground. So much of what I have written helps us reexamine what is "normal"; who decides what is "normal," what is human, what is "speech," what is "communication"; and how our understandings of the "social" contract, the faith, our community, or God have informed the decisions we have made both for and against the marginalized.

I would like to add one other voice to the many voices clamoring to be "heard"—the voice of Nelle Morton, one of the pioneer women theologians of the past century. I wrote at length about the theological concept of *Logos*, so prominent in the Christian scriptures, and of *dabar*, the Hebrew equivalent in the Hebrew scriptures. I cited sources within Christian tradition that believed those without the ability to speak oral "words" might be at risk of eternal damnation, as if the God who created them did not have the capacity to understand them! Yet these discursive thoughts were still couched in an old binary dualism: God talks, we listen. As the United Church of Christ says in its motto, "God is still speaking." Yes, but Morton rightfully turns this time-worn paradigm upside down when she writes about the long-overdue liberation of women from the patriarchy's historic and entrenched clutches.

Like her forbearer Eve, who is blamed for biting the "apple," Morton continues this act of insurrection by upsetting the theological applecart. Clothed in little more than a metaphorical fig leaf, Morton stands at the gate of Eden, not shamed, not subdued, challenging all the theologies that have been wielded against women over the ages, across cultures and religions and creeds. Standing in the full light of day, stepping forth from the shadows of sin and darkness, she challenges the Deity:

> A fundamental question now insinuates itself: Could the limiting imagery in the word Word—Logos—derive from a patriarchal way of perceiving and experiencing the universe? Would a more inclusive perceiving allow for persons to be heard into existence rather than spoken into existence? …Could it be that Logos-deified reduces communication to a one-way relationship—that of speaking—and bypasses the far more radical divine aspect of hearing?[1]

Reflecting on her involvement with other women, she states unreservedly that women have come into new speech simply because they were finally being heard by other women, listened to, encouraged. So she takes this powerful insight and applies it to the Divine: "In the beginning was not the Word. In the beginning was the hearing."[2] Thus, the divine act is hearing into speech rather than speaking into hearing. Morton concludes,

> Every liberation movement rises out of its bondage with a new speech. This has been so with women coming together, seeking to get in touch with our own stories and experiences which we have discovered welling up from within, from underneath, from out of our past, from out of our traditions rather than down from above. But to evoke our story to speech, women experience an imperative—a prior great Listening Ear…an ear that hears without interruption down through our defenses, cliche-filled language pretensions, evasions, pervasive hurts, angers, frustration, internalized stereotyped images until we experience at the lowest point of our lives that we are sustained. Women are literally hearing one another to speech. But the speech is our speech. It may come on stumblingly or boldly. But it is authentically our own.[3]

This simple yet profound term has been adopted by feminist theologians as one of their famous battle cries. Xochitl Alvizo, in her article, "Hearing Each Other to Speech in the Academy," expands on the event that caused this to happen.[4] Nelle Morton coined the feminist principle of "hearing to speech." Morton's new understanding of hearing and speaking came to her while she was with a group of women who gathered to tell their stories. As one woman shared her story—a story which at times reached points of excruciating pain—no one moved or interrupted, everyone seemed to be holding their breath. At the end, when the woman finally finished, she said, "You heard me. You heard me all the way—I have the strange feeling you heard me before I started."

If we truly understand that the "Other" doesn't have to be like us, that the "Other" isn't a threat and doesn't need to be "fixed," that we can trust the Holy Ground on which we all stand, and take off our shoes and sit with one another, allowing the Other to tell us their stories—whether in speech, in art, in music, in dance, in sign—we can reach the "Peaceable Kingdom" that is held out as our hope, that maybe is even faintly remembered as our past, where we delight in one another and revel in one another's uniqueness. It is thus appropriate to the hope and the challenge in the opening song, "Walls or Windows," by Judy Small: "The wall that stands between us can be a mirror too / When I look in the mirror, I see you."[5]

And let all the people say [sign] AMEN!

Notes

[1] Nelle Morton, *The Journey Is Home* (Boston: Beacon Press, 1986), 127-128.
[2] Ibid., 40.
[3] Ibid., 6.
[4] "Hearing Each Other to Speech in the Academy," *Feminism and Religion*, August 18, 2011.
[5] Judy Small, "Walls or Windows," *One Small Voice I the Crowd*, Crafty Maid Music, 1985.

Bibliography

Allport, Gordon. *The Nature of Prejudice*. 25th Anniversary Edition Paperback—Special Edition. New York: Basic Books, 1979.

Althaus-Reid, Marcella. *Indecent Theology: Theological Perversions in Sex, Gender and Politics*. London and New York: Routledge, 2000.

Althaus-Reid, Marcella, and Lisa Isherwood, *The Sexual Theologian: Essays on Sex, God and Politics*. New York: T & T Clark International, 2004.

An Account of the Origin and Progress of the Pennsylvania Institution of the Deaf and Dumb. Philadelphia: Harvard, 2009.

Baldwin, Neil. *Henry Ford and the Jews: The Mass Production of Hate*. Public Affairs, 2001.

Ballin, Albert. *The Deaf-Mute Howls*. Washington DC: Gallaudet University Press, 1998.

Baynton, Douglas C. *Forbidden Signs: American Culture and the Campaign Against Sign Language*. Chicago: University of Chicago Press, 1996.

———. "The Undesirability of Admitting Deaf Mutes. *U.S. Immigration Policy and Deaf Immigrants, 1882–1924*. Sign Language Studies 6, no. 4 (Summer 2006): 391–415.

Bonet, Juan Pablo. Summary of the letters and the art of teaching speech to the mute. Translation. 1620. A digital copy of Juan Pablo Bonet's "Reduction de las letras" (*Summary of the Letters and the Art of Teaching Speech to the Mute*) is available through Internet Archive, with a direct link to the work at archive.org. The Becker Medical Library has also discussed Bonet's work.

Buber, Martin. *I and Thou*. German, 1923; English reprint, Edinburgh: T&T Clark, 1937.

Chopp, Rebecca, and Mark Lewis Taylor, editors. *Reconstructing Christian Theology*. Minneapolis: Fortress Press, 1997.

Chorost, Michael. *Rebuilt: My Journey Back to the Hearing World*. USA: Mariner Books, 2005.

Cone, James. *A Black Theology of Liberation: Twentieth Anniversary Edition*. Maryknoll, NY: Orbis, 1990.

Cooper, Burton. "The Disabled God." *Theology Today*, 49, no. 2 (1992): 173–82.

Cruz, Laurence. "Eugenics Yields Dark Past." *Statesman Journal*. December 1, 2002.

Dimmock, A. F. *Cruel Legacy: An Introduction to the Record of Deaf People in History*. Edinburgh: Scottish Workshop Publications, 1993.

Dundes, Alan. *Holy Writ as Oral Lit: The Bible as Folklore*. Lanham, MD: Rowman and Littlefield, Publishers, Inc., 1999.

Dyer, Mary Heron. *Between the Deaf and Hearing Worlds: Blazing My Own Trail.* Journey Road Publishing, 2022.

Eiesland, Nancy L. *The Disabled God: Toward a Liberatory Theology of Disability.* Nashville: Abingdon Press, 1994.

Eisner, Will, and Umberto Eco. *The Plot: The Secret Story of the Protocols of the Elders of Zion.* W.W. Norton & Co., 2006.

Ellison, Marvin, and Sylvia Thorson-Smith, editors. *Body and Soul: Rethinking Sexuality as Justice-Love.* Cleveland: The Pilgrim Press, 2003.

Emerson, Ralph Waldo. "Concord Hymn." 1837.

Faderman, Lillian. *Odd Girls and Twilight Lovers: A History of Lesbian Life in Twentieth Century America.* Penguin Books, 1991.

Freud, Sigmund. *Three Contributions to the Theory of Sexuality: A monograph.* Leipzig and Vienna: Deuticke, 1905.

Gallo, Marcia. *Different Daughters: A History of the Daughters of Bilitis and the Rise of the Lesbian Rights Movement.* Carrol & Graf Publishers, 2006.

Goss, Robert E. *Queering Christ: Beyond Jesus Acted Up.* Cleveland: The Pilgrim Press, 2002.

Grant, Jacquelyn. *White Women's Christ and Black Women's Jesus: Feminist Christology and Womanist Response.* The American Academy of Religion, Atlanta, GA, 1989.

Greenberg, Joanna. *In This Sign.* New York: Henry Holt and Company, 1970.

Grose, Francis. *1811 Dictionary of the Vulgar Tongue: A Dictionary of Buckish Slang, University Wit, and Pickpocket Eloquence.* Republished by Cavalier Classics, 2015.

Heyward, Carter. *Our Passion for Justice.* Pilgrim Press, 1984.

———. *The Seven Deadly Sins of White Christian Nationalism: A Call to Action.* Rowland and Littlefield Publishers, 2022.

———. *Touching Our Strength: The Erotic as Power and the Love of God.* San Francisco: HarperCollins Publishing, 1989.

Houston, Jeanne Wakatsuki, and Sam Houston. *Farewell to Manzanar.* Houghton Mifflin, 2013.

Hull, John M. *In the Beginning There Was Darkness: A Blind Person's Conversation with the Bible.* London: SCM Press, 2001.

Johnson, David K. *The Lavender Scare: The Cold War Persecution of Gays and Lesbians in the Federal Government.* Reprint, University of Chicago Press, 2006.

Johnson, Jay Emerson. *Divine Communion: A Eucharistic Theology of Sexual Intimacy.* Church Publishing Incorporated, 2013.

———. *Peculiar Faith: Queer Theology for Christian Witness.* Seabury Books, 2014.

Jorgensen, Christine with Susan Stryker. *Christine Jorgensen: A Personal Biography*. New York: Bantam Books, 1967.

Kalilombe, Patrick A. *Doing Theology at the Grassroots: Theological Essays from the Grassroots*. Luviri Press, Malawi. 2008.

Katz, Jonathan Ned. *Gay American History: Lesbians and Gay Men in the U.S.A.* New York: Crowell, 1976.

King, Dean. *Skeletons in the Zahara: A True Story of Survival*. New York: Little Brown and Company, 2004.

Krafft-Ebing, Richard von. *Psychopathia Sexualis: The Classic Study of Deviant Sex*. Stuttgart: Verlag Von Ferdinand Enke, 1886.

Lane, Harlan. *The Mask of Benevolence: Disabling the Deaf Community*. San Diego, CA: DawnSign Press, 1999.

———. *When the Mind Hears: A History of the Deaf*. New York: Vintage Books, 1989.

Lettini, Gabriella. *Moral Injury: A Guidebook for Understanding and Engagement*. Boston: Beacon Press, 2021.

———. *Omosessualità*. 1999.

———. Co-written with Rita Nakashima Brock. *Soul Repair: Recovering from Moral Injury After the War*. Boston: Beacon Press, 2013.

Levinas, Emmanuel. *Ethics and Infinity: Conversations with Philippe Nemo*. Translated by Richard A. Cohen. Pittsburgh, PA: Duquesne University Press, 1995.

———. *Totality and Infinity: An Essay on Exteriority*. Translated by Alphonso Lingis. Pittsburgh, PA: Duquesne University Press, 1969.

Lewis, Hannah. *Deaf Liberation Theology*. Aldershot, England: Ashgate, 2007.

Lomicky, Carol, and Chuck Salestrom. *North Platte's Keith Blackledge: Lessons from a Community Journalist*. The History Press, 2021.

Lomicky, Carol S., Trudy C. De Goede et al. *Handbook for Research in Media Law*. Blackwell Pub Professional, 2005.

Lord, Albert. *Singer of Tales*. Cambridge, MA: Harvard University Press, 1960.

Louÿs, Pierre. *The Songs of Bilitis*. Paris, 1894.

Maher, Jane. *Seeing Language in Sign: The Work of William C. Stokoe*. Washington, DC: Gallaudet University Press, 1996.

McCloughry, R., and W. Morris. *Making a World of Difference: Christian Reflections on Disability*. London: SPCK, 2002.

Medhurst, Eleanor. *Unsuitable: A History of Lesbian Fashion*. Hurst Publishers: London, UK, 2024.

Melville, Herman. *Moby Dick*. Harper and Brothers, 1851.

Morris, Wayne. *Theology without Words: Theology in the Deaf Community*. Hampshire, England: Ashgate Publishing Limited, 2008.

Morton, Nelle. *The Journey Is Home*. Boston: Beacon Press, 1985.

———. *Embodiment: An Approach to Sexuality and Christian Theology*. Minneapolis: Augsburg Publishing House, 1978.

Oliveto, Karen. *Our Strangely Warmed Hearts: Coming Out to God's Call*. Nashville: Abingdon Press, 2018.

Padden, Carol, and Tom Humphries. *Inside Deaf Culture*. Cambridge, MA: Harvard University Press, 2005.

Parnell, Peter, and Justin Richardson. *And Tango Makes Three*. New York: Simon and Schuster, 2005.

Phelps-Roper, Megan. *Unfollow: A Memoir of Loving and Leaving the Westboro Baptist Church*. Farrar, Straus, and Giroux, 2019.

Plant, Richard. *The Pink Triangle: The Nazi War Against Homosexuals*. Washington, DC: New Republic Books, 1986.

Pope, Alexander. *An Essay on Criticism*. 1711.

Pui-lan, Kwok. *The Anglican Tradition from a Postcolonial Perspective*. White Plains, NW: Seabury Books, 2023.

Richardson, Justin, and Peter Parnell. *And Tango Makes Three*. Simon and Schuster, 2005.

Roughgarden, Joan. *Evolution's Rainbow: Diversity, Gender, and Sexuality in Nature and People*. Berkeley: University of California Press, 2004.

Rule, Jane. *Desert of the Heart*. 1964; reprint, Bella Books, 2005.

Russo, Vito. *The Celluloid Closet: Homosexuality in the Movies*, revised edition. New York: Harper and Row, 1987.

Ryan, Donna F., and John S. Schuchman, editors. *Deaf People in Hitler's Europe*. Washington DC: Gallaudet University Press, 2002.

Schein, Jerome D. *At Home among Strangers: Exploring the Deaf Community in the United States*. Washington DC: Gallaudet University Press, 1989.

Segovia, Fernando F. *Decolonizing Biblical Studies: A View from the Margins*. Maryknoll, NY: Orbis, 2020.

Shepard, Judy. *The Meaning of Matthew: My Son's Murder in Laramie, and a World Transformed*. Hudson Street Press, 2009.

Sound and Fury. Directed by Josh Aronson. Artistic License Films. 80 minutes. 2000.

Sound and Fury: Six Years Later. Directed by Josh Aronson. Aronson Films. 29 minutes. 2006.

Steinberg, Leo. *The Sexuality of Christ in Renaissance Art and in Modern Oblivion*. Chicago: The University of Chicago Press, 1983.

Stuart, Elizabath. *Gay and Lesbian Theologies: Repetitions with Critical Difference.* Hampshire, England: Ashgate Publishing Limited, 2003.

Tan, Amanda. "The Disabled Christ." *Transformation* 15, no. 4 (1998): 8-14.

Teagarden, Joan. *Evolution's Rainbow: Diversity, Gender, and Sexuality in Nature and People.* Berkeley: University of California Press, 2004.

Teal, Donn. *The Gay Militants.* New York: St. Martin's Press, 1971.

Thurman, Howard. *Jesus and the Disinherited.* 1949; reprint, Boston: Beacon Press, 1996.

Timmerman, Joan, *The Mardi Gras Syndrome: Rethinking Christian Sexuality.* New York: Crossroad, 1985.

Tropiano, Stephen. *The Prime-Time Closet: A History of Gays and Lesbians on TV.* New York: Applause Theatre and Cinema Books, 2002).

Ware, K. "The Spirituality of the Icon." In C. Jones et al., editors, *The Study of Spirituality.* London, 2000.

Winefield, Richard. *Never the Twain Shall Meet: The Communications Debate.* Washington DC: Gallaudet University Press, 1987.

Woodward, James. *How You Gonna Get to Heaven If You Can't Talk with Jesus? On Depathologizing Deafness.* Silver Spring, MD: T. J. Publishers, Inc., 1982.

www.ingramcontent.com/pod-product-compliance
Lightning Source LLC
Chambersburg PA
CBHW070937180426
43192CB00039B/2311